"Boards by MelFran is one of my favorite Instagram accounts! Every time I see one of Melissa's posts in my feed I immediately become inspired to create a gorgeous arrangement and host a party! Her work is creative, beautiful, artful and delicious. I was thrilled to see Melissa release *Boards & Bites*. Not only is the layout of the book stunning, but she makes building each yummy creation easy and actionable. I love the way she breaks down the science of a charcuterie board, providing a step-by-step guide on how to create color-schemed boards and themed displays. Not only will you be impressed with how your boards look by mimicking what Melissa teaches you, your tastebuds will be overjoyed!"

—Melissa Coulier, photographer and visual branding consultant

"Melissa's boards and bites are works of art. There are so many colors and textures, they scream celebration. But beyond looking pretty they are also very well-thought-out flavor pairings, easy-to-follow instructions, and an understanding of cheese that goes beyond the norm."

—Warren Katz, corporate executive chef and lover of cheese

"*Boards & Bites* is the perfect go-to board guide for your next get together. Melissa breaks all of the need-to-know info down so that it is easy to follow and easy to create a beautiful, colorful board of your own. In addition to boards, her recipes are sure to wow and are perfect to serve when you host your next get together!"

—Alaura Berry from @berry&theboards, visual and food stylist

"Melissa's boards fill my heart with joy every time I see them on my Instagram feed. You can tell immediately the meticulousness and passion she has for her craft. Watching her create her stunning boards inspire me to hone my own craft. This book is going to forever live on my counter so I can recreate every design!"

—Tess Levin, culinary comedian, creator of the food blog *Fluff Cups*, and creator/host of *Sweet Talks* on YouTube

Boards & Bites

Copyright © 2022 by Melissa Francis.
Published by Yellow Pear Press, a division of Mango Publishing Group, Inc.

Cover Design: Elina Diaz
Cover Photo: Melissa Francis
Illustrations: Emane Henderson
Interior Photos: Melissa Francis, Dave Novotney, & Melissa Coulier
Layout & Design: Elina Diaz

For permission requests, please contact the publisher at:
Mango Publishing Group
2850 S Douglas Road, 4th Floor
Coral Gables, FL 33134 USA
info@mango.bz

For special orders, quantity sales, course adoptions and corporate sales, please email the publisher at sales@mango.bz. For trade and wholesale sales, please contact Ingram Publisher Services at customer.service@ingramcontent.com or +1.800.509.4887.

Boards & Bites: Food Styling and Homemade Recipes for Elegant Party Planning

Library of Congress Cataloging-in-Publication number: 2022942978
ISBN: (print) 978-1-68481-063-5 (eBook) 978-1-68481-064-2
BISAC category code: CKB003000, COOKING / Courses & Dishes / Appetizers

Printed in China

Boards & Bites

Food Styling and Homemade Recipes for Elegant Party Planning

Melissa Francis

yellow pear  press

CORAL GABLES

Table of Contents

INTRODUCTION

I am extremely fortunate to have grown up with a family who values spending time together, honors traditions, and, arguably most importantly, enjoys food. The norm at our house is my mom's side, my dad's side, and family friends come to enjoy delicious food and have a fantastic time. My father Kevin was born in India, then moved to Toronto, Canada, and then to California, USA. My mother Kim was born and raised in California. My parents appeared to have polar opposite upbringings, but somehow their relationship melded two families into the vibrant multicultural one we are today. I've come to realize that I am extremely fortunate to have a family where all sides get along and share similar values because it created, and continues to create, loving memories.

At our house, planning and prepping to host a gathering is a multi-day, maybe even week-long production of cleaning, prepping, decorating, and cooking. Being raised where this was the norm, I subconsciously picked up on the tips and tricks that made hosting run smoothly. Every memory of those get-togethers has left me feeling blessed and full of fond memories.

Even as a kid, I wanted to take a more active role in hosting these events. First, I became the family photographer and created festive traditions like our "Annual Easter Egg Toss" or our "Christmas Cookie Decorating Contest" (the winner receives twenty dollars, so let's just say frosting flies, people!). I wanted to cook, but with my dad doing the grilling or meat smoking and my mom doing everything else, there wasn't really a place for me. Until the fateful day I created my first charcuterie board, and the rest was history.

To tell you the truth, I started creating boards exclusively for my brother Nick (who was always Nicky to me). He was my original guinea pig. I will single-handedly take credit for forcing Nicky to try new foods and expand his palate. Nowadays, Nicky rarely gets a board made just for him; if he is lucky, he gets some spare prosciutto. When I started making boards, I loved witnessing him try new foods and seeing how happy my creations made him feel. Making food for others is an act of love in my eyes.

During my last internship at Rancho Los Amigos National Rehabilitation Hospital, while I was getting my master's degree to become a speech and language pathologist, I had an epiphany. I realized the

insanely positive impact making food for others can have. I worked with a young patient who had recently experienced a traumatic brain injury. He had mentioned that his favorite cereal was Trix™, so he and I created a recipe incorporating it. We only had a microwave, so we came up with a microwave-friendly recipe for crispy treats using this cereal. Though not the most scrumptious treat, making them together was fun, and sharing them with others and seeing all those smiles and excitement was an exceptionally positive experience. At that moment, I thought about how something so small can bring so much joy and be the highlight of someone's day. From then on, I decided to make as many people smile as those treats did. Outside of my speech and language pathology work, I found that presenting, receiving, or even being a guest at an event with a well-thought-out charcuterie board can set the mood for the event and provide a cherished memory.

Ever since I did my first charcuterie board, I fell in love with the idea of creating something beautiful that brought people together. I finally had my rightful designated job at my family get-togethers as the charcuterie board creator. Slowly but surely, word spread, and I started creating boards for others, posting Instagram photos, and sharing my board journey. My first round of boards was for a neighbor's birthday party. The nerves I felt were unreal, but I felt truly honored that someone trusted me to make five—I repeat: five—boards for an event.

As a board lover, I continue trying new styling techniques and working on perfecting old ones. As a host, I strive to plan, be prepared, and always keep my guests' happiness at the top of my priority list. Through this book, I can share the sophisticated end products of many hours of trial and error. Boards by Melfran has taught me so much while bringing me closer to my family and friends. I remember a few loved ones saying, "You should write a cookbook." I giggled and sarcastically replied, "Maybe one day." Well, I guess they knew something I did not because here we are.

When brainstorming what I wanted this book to be about, I pondered what makes Boards by Melfran unique. Mostly, I strive to use bright, vibrant colors in an eye-catching and uncommon way. Chic and classy, always delicious but notable and worth remembering, are qualities that, I think, make my boards unique.

These pages contain the tips, tricks, and strategies that make a board chic, colorful, and the center of attention. I hope you, dear reader, not only learn a thing or two about how to enhance and elevate your boards but that you also enjoy the heart, soul, and family love these pages contain.

❀ Charcuterie: cold cooked meats

❀ Crudités: assortment of raw vegetables

THIRTEEN RULES FOR THE KITCHEN

Before we dive into it, I want to lay some ground rules that I try to live by in the kitchen. My lucky number has been number thirteen for as long as I can remember. While the number 13 is unlucky for most, when I was little, my family told me that if/when I ever saw the number 13 it was my granny checking in. Granny is my great-grandmother, who unfortunately passed away before I met her, but I have been told by countless people that we are insanely similar. Since then, 13 has always brought me comfort—enough comfort that I have it tattooed on my foot (don't tell Kfran, a.k.a. my dad).

Here is the breakdown of my "Thirteen Rules for the Kitchen":

1. No Board Is Ever Too Big

In my house, the standard was never "less is more." Instead, it was "more is better." If you took a survey of every person who had ever been a guest at my home, I truly believe no one would say they left hungry. Food can be and mean many things to people. For me, my family, and guests, food has always made everyone feel insanely comfortable. In my book (OMG, literally in *my* book!), one of the greatest compliments you can receive as a host is that your guests feel comfortable in your home. Comfort directly correlates to food because, for most people, food is comfort. Food is a topic of discussion and an all-inclusive sensory experience. I was taught and continue to practice that ensuring every guest has enough food to enjoy is and always should be a priority, so no board is ever too big. Even if it is too big, has anyone ever complained about having leftovers? Not me.

2. There Is No Such Thing as "Too Much" Garnish

Oh, garnish! Garnishing my food is one of my favorite parts to any recipe or board. To me, garnish time is the time to let your personality shine through and shine bright, baby! The traditional definition of garnish is to decorate or embellish. The Boards by Melfran definition of garnish is to "decorate or embellish to the nines and to let it be your self-expression." My love for garnish stems from the fact that you can create an entire vibe, color scheme, or theme with garnish. Utilizing a plethora of garnishes creates endless combinations of textures, colors, and dimensions. Don't stress if utilizing garnish overwhelms you—there's an entire chapter dedicated to the art of garnish starting on p. 74.

Garnish: decorate or embellish

3. No Shame in the Semi-Homemade Game

I am the biggest self-advocate of "work smarter, not harder." If a recipe calls for dough, go to the store and buy yourself some premade dough, unless you enjoy making dough (or any food, for that matter) from scratch. If that's the case, you do you! I discovered my love for creating semi-homemade recipes when I made cupcakes for my friend's birthday. I always made chocolate cupcakes from a box with vanilla frosting from a can. By using store-bought mixes, I could use the time I saved to focus on embellishing and customizing the cupcakes. I always added in extra chocolate chips because why not? And, of course, I made custom frosting colors and swirls based on their aesthetic. Long story short: Make your life easier. Work smarter, not harder; cut corners where it does not matter.

4. Save Yourself the Potential Sogginess and Place the Crackers on the Side

Disclaimer: No hate or judgment for putting crackers on a board! I am too much of a paranoid type-A human being to not hyper-fixate on the crackers potentially being soggy. I love to pack in the veggies and fresh fruit, which all produce moisture—and the fear of me or someone I care about expecting to bite into a crunchy cracker, but taking a huge bite into soggy mush (I know you know the texture I am talking about) makes me cringe. Besides, being a paranoid, type-A human being, I am also a texture addict. I love all the textures different foods provide and feel it is crucial to keep the crackers at their intended texture. Just to reiterate, no judgment or hate to you if you put crackers on your boards—who knows, maybe you have created a fool-proof method to avoid sogginess. If that is the case, please contact me immediately.

5. Cooking Is Trial and Error

Cooking is trial and error. Unfortunately, that is just the harsh reality of cooking. Trust me, I know the feeling of getting all the ingredients, following a recipe to a T, and then looking confused at the final product. Like, *what*? Or even worse, the final product looks right, but you give it a taste, and you are like, "*What?*" We have all been there, but do not give up! It is important to try it out, self-assess what went wrong or what you would do differently, and then give it another go! Who knows, maybe what you thought would be an "error" turns into something amazing. Just do not give up!

6. "You Can Tell a Good Cook by the Size of Their Spice Cabinet"

This quote came directly from my great-grandma Taylor. I hate to admit it, but she would not be happy with my semi-homemade rule because this woman knew how to bake and had the best homemade recipes. That is beside the point, though. When you open a spice cabinet and you're instantly confronted with a blended aroma of different spices, you know they are cooking up some good stuff. Do not be afraid to experiment and try different flavor profiles. Mix it up, and pair spices with different spices. It is important to remember that everyone has different taste buds, and making sure you develop your favorite spice combinations should be priority number one.

7. Trust Your Intuition

Trust yourself. You know more than you think. Every oven is calibrated differently; not every measurement will be perfect, no matter how hard you try; the perfect cook time for something will not necessarily be *your* perfect cook time. Take pasta, for instance. I love myself some al dente pasta. Some may even say I enjoy *crunchy* pasta (it is just al dente, though), but just because I cut the cook time on the box in half does not mean you have to. It is crucial that while you are "chef-ing" it up, you develop self-awareness and pay attention to the cues your food provides you throughout the cooking process. If your house is suddenly filled with the savory aroma of garlic bread, take a second, check on it and make sure it is browning to perfection and not charred to a crisp. If you feel like the cook time the recipe recommends is too long, trust yourself and set your timer for less. Even though it may not feel like it, you know best.

8. Garlic...the Limit Does Not Exist

This may be controversial, but I truly live by this rule. If a recipe calls for a certain amount of garlic, you better believe I am doubling it—at least. When working with garlic, there is a hierarchy of potency. Garlic powder is the least potent and has the longest shelf life. Roasted garlic and minced garlic in olive oil are middle of the road when it comes to potency. The most potent is always fresh garlic. Be conscious of the type of garlic you use and how potent it may be. As long as you are aware, go crazy with it. In my mind, garlic adds nothing but intense, amazing flavor.

9. Plan Ahead and Don't Stress

Whether you are hosting or bringing a board to someone's home, the last thing you want to be is rushing, frazzled, and stressed. All those negative emotions will impact your experience, and that is never the goal. Set yourself up for success to maximize happiness and minimize stress. If you plan on creating a board or recipe (or anything in between), take a few moments a few days prior to plan out the items you need. Make a list and give yourself enough time to go to the store, get ready, and feel good. Planning can be tedious and daunting, but trust me, in the end, you will thank yourself for doing the prep work—especially later when you are sipping on a glass of wine accompanied by a board and laughing with your friends and family.

10. Let Your Creativity Flow

Creativity allows you to bring what is going on in your head to life. I would say this rule has two main parts: the creative part and the letting-it-flow part. Many recipes or ideas have popped into my mind randomly, and I have learned to write them down before I forget. Creativity comes to me throughout the day; for others, there may be a time and place for the creativity to flow. Time for the second part of this rule: letting it flow. If you think of an idea, recipe, design, or just about anything, do not be afraid to try it out and see what happens! Maybe it will be a hot mess, or maybe it will be a stroke of creative genius—only experimenting will tell. Another important thing to note is while you are letting that creativity flow, do not be afraid to change your mind or plan. Both are part of the creative process.

11. Mistakes Are Learning Opportunities

If you cook out of the box and try new recipes you have never tried before, cut yourself some cheese—I mean, slack. You will inevitably make mistakes, but it doesn't matter as long as you learn from them. As stated above, cooking is trial and error, so mistakes will happen. When they do, take a second and figure out when and why your recipe took a turn for the worse.

12. Your Eyes Eat First

These days, "phone eats first," but you get the idea. Vision is one of the first sensations to activate when you anticipate enjoying a meal. If your food is colorful, vibrant, and appealing, you will be more invested and excited to eat. If your recipe looks pretty and detailed, as a chef, you will be proud and happy with the results.

13. Love What You Are Making, Creating, and Doing

As I have gone through the process of creating recipes, boards, and everything in between, I have tried to prioritize loving what I am making, creating, and doing. Sometimes I have gone through waves of burnout on my cooking journey, which is okay. When these periods arise, I take a moment to relax, regroup, and go back to the drawing board. I try to focus on letting my creativity flow and seeing what happens. I want your cooking experience to be positive and filled with fond memories and cherished laughs, so if you stop loving what you are making, creating, and doing, take a step back and focus on finding what you love again.

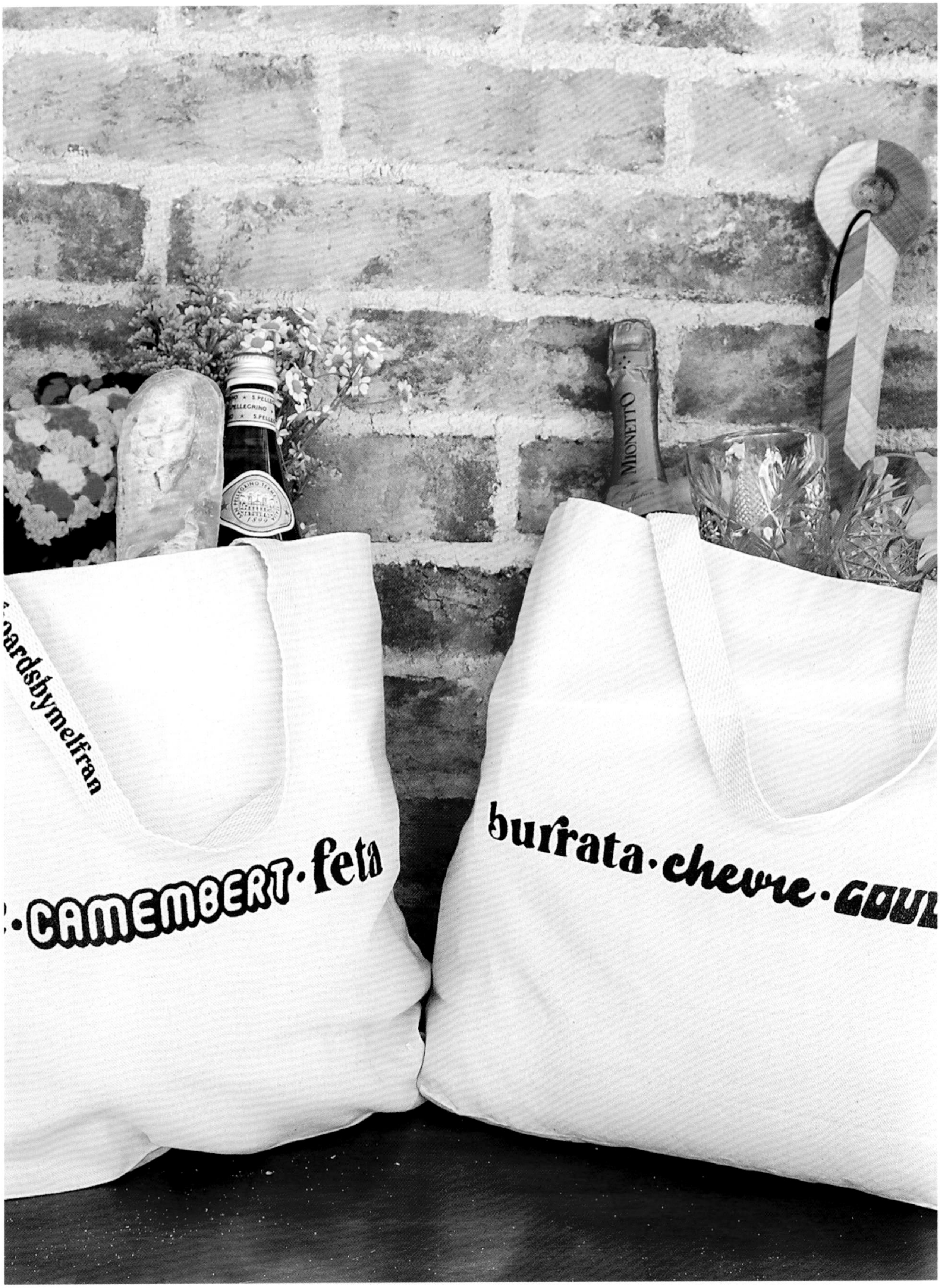
S.PELLEGRINO
MIONETTO
CAMEMBERT · feta
burrata · chevre ·

THE PLANNING & PREP

Let's Make a Plan

Put down the board! Before we get ahead of ourselves, let's take a step back. Creating a charcuterie board, especially a chic one, can be stress-inducing and intimidating. It requires proper brainstorming and planning. After multiple (stressful) trials and tribulations, I have come up with the perfect plan you can use. In all fairness, I must admit I am the designated planner in my friend group and the group member or coworker who sets up the Google drive and gets everyone's phone numbers to create a group chat. I hate being frazzled and stressed, so I have learned to be prepared for all potential problems that may occur. Due to the nature of my day job as a speech and language pathologist, I am constantly planning and envisioning the future. When working with my patients and students, the importance of creating a plan has become extremely clear, as is the implementation and execution of the plan. Planning and prepping for anything in life, including creating a beautiful board, requires executive functioning skills. In a nutshell, executive functioning is the boss of your brain. It's the management system that allows you to prepare, initiate, execute, and complete a plan to achieve your goals. The basic skills of executive functioning that are integral to cooking include adaptable thinking, time management, and organization. To get started, you need to start thinking.

1. Look into your crystal ball and start thinking: What do you want to do? Host a dinner party? Head to a picnic?

2. What do you want your charcuterie board to look like when it's done?

3. Now, take your envisioned board and work backward: What steps and sequence are needed to achieve your envisioned board?

4. What items do you need to create your board?

Above are the steps I take before creating just about anything. This thought process helps me feel ready to rock and roll. Remember, prepping a thoughtful and beautiful board requires implementing executive functioning skills to set yourself up for success.

Once I get my basic concept mapped out in my head, I like to focus on answering the following questions:

1. How many people does this board need to feed?

2. When will this board be enjoyed?

3. Is there a theme or color scheme that this board needs to fit?

4. Do guests have dietary restrictions that need to be taken into consideration?

5. Do any other tasks need to be completed besides the board? If so, how will that impact my time?

For all you detail-oriented individuals, now is your time to shine. It's time to get to the nitty-gritty details. Take a moment and ask yourself these questions.

1. What shape/style board do I want to use? (check pg. 55-60 for ideas)

2. What types of cheeses and charcuterie do I envision on this board?

3. What fruits and veggies do I envision? (Remember to consider what foods will be in season and check pg. 40 for season produce.)

4. Are there any recipes for spreads or dips I want to make to add to my board? If yes, what ingredients will I need?

5. Are there any show-stopping recipes or sides I want to create? If yes, what will I need?

Once you have a solid vision in your head of your picture-perfect board, it is list time!

List

Cheese
- boursin
- irish cheddar
- fresh mozz
- brie

charcuterie
- salami
- proscuitto

fruit
- pineapple
- clemintines
- red grapes
- strawerries
- berries

veggies
- cucumbers
- tomatoes
- garlic

misc.
- olives
- jam

Grocery List

Now that your vision is complete, it's time to make your list! I have learned the hard way, especially when I am in a rush, that if I don't make a list, it is inevitable that something will be forgotten. And if the worst should happen, trust in your ability to improvise! One time I forgot to get one of my staple cheeses, an Irish cheddar. At this point, I was a creature of habit and always did a salami river, cucumber river, and an Irish cheddar river. But I did not get the cheddar and had to completely change the board I had envisioned. In a stressed, panicked state, I had a thought to make a brie river. It ended up coming out amazing, and it's safe to say I am now a huge supporter of the brie river. As cliche as it sounds, everything happens for a reason. Forgetting something forces you to be flexible, creative, and potentially come up with something amazing. While these times were stressful, they turned out to be happy accidents.

So, the moral of the story is: Plan while you can, but if you forget something, it is not the end of the world. Make a list and save yourself the stress.

I present to you the "tragi-brie" that became "brie-tiful." These photos were the products of my forgotten Irish cheddar and why I continue to believe that everything happens for a reason.

Below is the board list that I refer to in my notes app on my phone at all times because it has all my go-to items and essentials. Before we get into the list, it is important to understand the differences between soft and hard cheeses. Soft cheeses may be made from various types of milk like cow, goat, or sheep, and traditionally have a higher moisture content. Soft cheese is unripened and made by coagulating milk proteins with acid. Hard cheese is also made from a wide variety of milk and is aged (ripened) by coagulating milk proteins with rennet and culture acids.

 Rennet: enzymes that trigger coagulation in milk proteins

Cheeses	Charcuterie	Fruits	Crudités	Additional
Soft Cheeses: • Goat cheese • Brie **Hard Cheeses:** • Irish cheddar • Gouda • Blue cheese	Salami Prosciutto Hard salami	Clementines Blueberries Strawberries Raspberries Blackberries Grapes	Cucumber Tomatoes	Honey Jam Mustard

When I started creating boards, I frequented my local grocery stores and supermarkets. As I got more confident and comfortable with the items I used regularly, I branched out and tried more local specialty shops and farmers markets. Specialty markets have such a fond place in my heart because they tend to be mom-and-pop shops full of delicious and one-of-a-kind products. The first speciality shop I went to was a family-owned olive oil shop. The owners let me try their rich olive oil, flavorful balsamic, and I left with a full stomach of olives—so delicious. Typically, produce from the farmers market is free from pesticides and preservatives, which, in my opinion, truly enhances the tastes and increases freshness. It has become my weekly routine to visit farmers markets for my veggies, specifically the most crisp and peppery arugula, and some rare fruit, like passion fruit. If you can check out and purchase from your local farmers markets, I recommend it.

Pro Tip: If time and schedules allow, I encourage taking multiple trips to the store, so you can dedicate one trip to the creation of your chic charcuterie board. Juggling your charcuterie board list and your weekly shopping is doable but can be tedious. When I need to grab my board produce and regular groceries at the same time, I create two lists so I have a literal visual cue to separate my items.

Serving Size

Growing up and still to this day, my house is the "hosting household," so I only know one way to host a party: It must have a *ton* of food. The Francis house was the house where people came and ate a ton of appetizers, a delicious main course, and my aunt's delicious desserts. My aunt makes peanut butter cereal treats with a chocolate drizzle that I routinely steal before the main course has even been served. After the party is over, family and friends gather up their containers and make claims on what leftovers they are taking home. Games are great and movies are entertaining, but let's be real, the crowd-pleaser is always the food. Ensuring you have enough food to leave your loved ones happy and satisfied should always be the goal. The following chart will help ensure your guests have fun and feel full.

	Appetizer per person	Main Spread per person
Cheese	1.5–2.0 oz (42.5–57 grams)	3.0–4.5 oz (85–127.5 grams)
Charcuterie (a.k.a. salami, prosciutto, capicola, etc.)	1.5–2.5 oz (42.5–71 grams)	2.5–4 oz (71–113 grams)
Fruit	3–4 oz (85–113 grams)	4–6 oz (113–170 grams)
Crudités (a.k.a. veggies)	2–3 oz (57–85 grams)	3–5 oz (85–142 grams)
Additions (a.k.a. honey, jam, mustard, etc.)	1.5–2.5 Tbsp (42.5–71 grams)	2.5–4 Tbsp (71-113 grams)
Carbs	1.0–2.5 oz (42.5–57 grams)	2.5–3.o oz (71–85 grams)

As you become more comfortable and accustomed to curating chic charcuterie boards, you will naturally develop the intuition to know how much of each item you will need.

Time Is of the Essence

There is no worse feeling than being the frazzled host or a late, stressed guest rushing through the door with a disheveled charcuterie board. I am a huge believer in planning ahead to reduce stress, so you can create something beautiful and focus on enjoying the occasion.

Below is a basic timeline I recommend following to set yourself up for success.

One week prior to event	Make your plan (refer to pg. 25) for details. **Pro Tip** (brought to you by my mom): Make a list of guests to help you visualize who is expected to come and if they have any special needs/requests like food allergies, dietary restrictions, etc. Schedule when you will be able to head to the store.
Four to five days prior	If you plan to head to the store twice, you can always get your cheeses and charcuterie earlier in the week. I frequently take multiple trips to the store and recommend breaking up your list (if possible) to alleviate the stress of a lengthy list. I tend to break up my list by categories like meats, cheeses, and crackers because they have a longer shelf life. During my second trip I will focus on the produce like fruits, vegetables, and floral and herb garnishes. **Pro Tip:** Always pick up a few of the same item to check the expiration dates. There have been countless times when I pick up one cheese and it has a different date than the cheese next to it.

Two to three days prior	Life gets busy and I understand that. You will want to head to the store as close to the date of the event as possible so your produce will be the freshest. **Pro Tip:** Always take a second to investigate your produce. I know it can be tedious, but take it from me: there is nothing worse than opening what looked to be the most beautiful batch of strawberries to find a moldy one smack dab in the middle. While at the store, I also recommend grabbing whatever fresh floral or herb garnishes you will need. See pg. 78 for tips on keeping your herbs and florals looking fresh and vibrant.
One to two days prior	Prepare any recipes needed for your board and store in airtight containers overnight. If you need every second on the day of the event/occasion, you can always: Pre-fold your salami (store in an airtight container; I add an extra layer of plastic wrap to lock in all the freshness) Wash and dry your produce (store with a paper towel inside to absorb any excess moisture)
Same day	The day is here, and it's time to assemble your board. If you can fit the entire charcuterie board in the fridge, you can truly make your board at any time. Please make sure you have the fridge space to store your board. When making your board before the event, you will want to securely wrap the board in plastic wrap and store it in the fridge until you are ready to serve.

Picnic Essentials

So, you've decided to take your charcuterie party outside. I've got you covered. During my last semester of graduate school, my friend group and I decided to celebrate the end of the term with picnics and wine tastings! Around five o'clock, we would head to the park by campus, set up our blankets, and enjoy wine and a Melfran creation. These regular picnics allowed me to be creative and learn what small details make a gathering run smoothly to ensure everyone is happy.

Each week, one person was the designated "sommelier" and brought a different wine for the group to try and rate. My little secret and sad truth is that my wine picks were always based on how cute the label was—don't tell anyone. This was a fun and interactive way to try new things (a.k.a. wine), be outside, and enjoy time with friends.

After much trial and error, I developed the picnic essentials to ensure you are happy, full, and clean!

Here is everything you will need to have the best chic charcuterie-inspired picnic:

The Cute Stuff	The Essentials	Keep It Tidy
Picnic basket Blankets (bring two in case the ground is damp) Fresh flowers Wine glasses	Wine opener Cutlery Napkins Plates Your favorite tote to hold everything in	Wipes Zip-top bags (for any leftovers) Trash bag

Now that all the planning, shopping, and prepping are complete, it is time to rock and roll and make the best board you can imagine. As creating boards became a regular occurrence, so did the planning, shopping, and prepping. Honestly, even though I am a planner at heart, the real fun begins now! My passion is in the process of creating, and the time has finally come. Time to pick the board back up and get to work!

ANATOMY & AESTHETIC OF A CHARCUTERIE BOARD

This chapter aims to give you a quick and clean overview of the anatomy and aesthetic of creating a board. As many of you probably did, I took anatomy in high school and did not think much of it. It was not until graduate school, when I had to learn the anatomy of the brain and swallowing mechanisms, that I comprehended the importance of a solid foundational understanding to build from. I am not saying the anatomy of a charcuterie board is like the anatomy of a brain whatsoever; rather, I think it is important to build a solid base of knowledge before getting into the details.

This chapter will also delve into the different types of charcuterie, serving sizes, and my step-by-step method for creating a board.

Seasons of Charcuterie

As the months go by and seasons change, so does the produce. If you are creating boards anytime, anywhere, rain or shine, always consider what produce is in season. When a fruit or vegetable is in season, it is at its peak freshness. Harvest time is based on the time of year and location in which you live. Many fruits and vegetables are available year-round due to modern technology and worldwide shipping. The benefit to focusing on "in season" food, however, is that it is fresh, at its peak deliciousness, and abundant, resulting in lower prices.

Using seasonal fruit and veggies, you can naturally incorporate the seasonal colors into your board. For example, pomegranates and chestnuts are dark and rich in color, perfect for boards curated during the winter season. Fresh figs and melons are so bright and fresh, just like summer.

Here are some seasonal items I gravitate toward and try to include in my boards each season:

Fall	Winter	Spring	Summer
Pomegranates	Pomegranates	Kumquats	Figs
Apples	Kumquats	Nectarines	Peaches
Pears	Citrus	Watermelon	Mangoes
Cranberries	Chestnuts	Apricots	Plums
Goldenberries		Pineapples	Melons
Persimmons			

When looking for seasonal produce, check what is populous in your area. You can always search online or ask your local produce connoisseur at your farmers market or grocery store.

Fall

Winter

Spring

Summer

Pro Tip (brought to you by my father Kevin, a.k.a. Kfran): Here's how to pick a one in a melon watermelon.

One day my dad texted the family group chat, asking if anyone needed anything from the store. I sarcastically looked at my mom and asked, "Do you think dad can get a good watermelon?" We laughed, and I texted, asking for a watermelon. To my pleasant surprise, my dad came home with one of the most delicious watermelons I have ever had. I apologized and admitted to him that I asked him to get a watermelon as a joke because I did not believe in his fruit selection abilities. Ever since that day, Kfran has been the designated watermelon man. At one point, he was picking up two watermelons a week for my house and five other watermelons for other family members. Kfran has agreed to share his watermelon secrets and here they are.

Kfran's Watermelon Tips:

1. Look at the spot where the watermelon lay on the ground. It should be a creamy yellow.

2. Look for spidering (little brown web-like lines). The spidering is caused by bee pollination and the more webbing, the sweeter the watermelon will be.

3. The pattern should be defined. Focus on a watermelon with a strong and consistent dark green and pastel yellow striped pattern.

4. Rounder is better than longer (longer watermelon means less sweet at the ends).

5. The watermelon stem should be dried out and brown.

6. Pick your top five watermelons and lift each. The heaviest is the least watery and most firm.

Types of Charcuterie

One of the best things about charcuterie is you can use anything from butcher paper to a mason jar to curate a beautiful and unique creation. By trying out different vessels and containers, you can find what you like and don't like. I have realized charcuterie cones are cute and fun but drive me nuts. Don't get me wrong, I still make them and love them, but I find the small space to be limiting to my creativity. I found that my true love lies in creating larger boards and grazing tables.

My first true grazing table was for one of my graduate school professor's birthdays. I was fortunate that my professor gave me creative freedom and had full confidence in me to create something out of this world. After many hours of planning, preparation, and folding salami, my assistant (a.k.a. my mom) and I packed up and were ready to tackle the table. Once the butcher paper was rolled out, it was all a blur because I was in the zone. After about two hours, the masterpiece was complete. Once the last dried citrus and rosemary were placed, I took 413 photographs (literally). I didn't want to leave my creation. It was my baby. Of course, I left...eventually!

To highlight the endless charcuterie possibilities I created a table to lay it out for you.

Boards	It all starts with a board! Boards are the most versatile and commonly used vessel to house your charcuterie creations. Boards are fantastic because they come in all shapes, sizes, and colors.	
Grazing Tables	Get out the butcher paper! A grazing table is going to give you the *wow* factor. Roll out butcher paper to your desired length and start creating! The butcher paper is so simple and easy, and it truly gives you a blank canvas to let your creativity go wild. You can always add crates or cake tiers for some height and dimension. **Pro Tip:** I like to pre-make two to four different boards to ease my stress and simply place them on the table and work around them. It looks seamless and seriously relieves you of so much stress.	
Cones	The perfect hand-held single serving of charcuterie! Charcuterie cones can be tricky to assemble, so you need to focus on items that are tall and sturdy. My tall and sturdy go-to items include a caprese skewer, fruit skewer, and folded salami skewer. Because a cone requires a person holding it to be successfully eaten (as opposed to a board that can be set safely on a table), you must make sure what is in the cone can hold its own and is as sturdy as possible.	

Boats	After I dabbled with charcuterie cones, I stumbled across the concept of charcuterie boats. In terms of creative convenience, I prefer boats to cones. However, in terms of cuteness, I cannot decide. Charcuterie boats are easier to create in because they are stable on their own and have more surface area. My charcuterie boat go-to items include a salami rose, Persian cucumber, caprese skewer, and clementines.	
Plates	A charcuterie plate is simplistic but still sophisticated. Utilizing a plate is good for small gatherings it is more manageable, and budget conscious. For a charcuterie plate, I like to focus on showcasing one to two unique cheeses. Not your run-of-the-mill cheddar, but maybe something fancier like a Spanish Manchego or camembert. As you can see, this plate—despite its small size—still possesses the iconic salami, cucumber, and cheese river! This trifecta can be used and enjoyed in any size at any time.	
Food Storage Containers	Using a container makes transportation and storage a breeze. A container can be similar to a plate in terms of being smaller—making it more of a small group serving size and budget-friendly. To add a personal touch, I love to use vintage containers to create an old-timey feel. This container showcases one cheese and one meat, accompanied by fruits and a cool cucumber.	

Recipe-Focused	A recipe-focused charcuterie presentation will feature one of the dishes presented in the "Semi-Homemade Showstoppers" chapter. This kind of presentation has a recipe as the star of the show, accompanied by a smaller board that revolves around your showstopper. This is a crudités board featuring the showstopper: Basil & White Bean Spread (pg. 111).	
Themed	A themed board comes into play during the holidays, special occasions, or anything along those lines. If you are creating a themed board, you want to make sure you are conscious of a few things: 1. Does the theme have signature colors? If yes, you will want to stick with those colors and make sure the garnish also focuses on those colors. Imagine a '70s-themed party—you will want your board to focus on highlighting bright oranges and greens, turquoise, sunshine yellows, warm browns, and purples. 2. Are there any designs or shapes you can use to ensure the theme translates well? For example, if you want to do a Disney-themed board, you can include Mickey Mouse's head shape throughout the board. 3. What types of food may play along with your theme? For example, if you are doing a board for a tailgate you may want to use more mustards, meats, or maybe even soft pretzels. This is a California-themed board. The board is shaped like the state of CA, which is fun. There are three cheeses on this board, all of which are handcrafted on the coast of California.	

Step-by-Step Food Styling Framework

1. Rivers

When creating a charcuterie board, the first thing I start with is my salami river (or my cucumber river if it's a veggie party). By placing the salami river first, I can create a fun curvy shape that will give my board structure. The river is important. It is basically the skeleton of your board, so take your time to place it and feel free to play around the shape.

2. Center Cheese

My next step is to put down my center point cheese. This is almost *always* a round cheese; typically, it is a wheel of brie or sweet and nutty goat cheese. I try to find a curve in my river that is somewhat centered and go for it. If there isn't a curve, I place my center cheese down and reshape my river to perfectly hug my center cheese.

My go-to centerpieces include:

- Sun Spread (pg. 108)
- Brie (pg. 97 & 101)
- Goat cheese (pg. 120 & 123)

3. River Time...Again

Now, I add my cucumber and cheese rivers. Cucumber has become a must-have on my boards because of the amazing color it gives and the fresh crunch it adds. Many people have told me their perfect bite is a fresh, crisp cucumber topped with sweet and nutty goat cheese.

Next up is the cheese river. I gravitate toward using a cheese that is easily sliced into triangles. For me, this is either brie or a cheddar of some sort.

The trifecta of the salami, cucumber, and cheese all next to one another creates a great base of colors that work well together.

4. Focal Points

Next, add your larger items. This includes anything in containers (spreads, honey, jam, balsamic vinegar, mustards, etc.). If you have large wedges of cheese that are best kept whole, like blue cheese or soft cheeses, you should place those next.

Spread the Love

Using spreads and soft cheeses allows your guests to add their desired amount for each bite. My go-tos for spreadable goodness includes:

- Sun Spread (pg. 108)

- Basil & White Bean Spread (pg. 111)

Cheeses

Hard cheeses give you creative freedom in terms of styling. My favorite ways to display hard cheeses are with triangles in a river and natural crumbles in the rind.

Accessories

Honey

Add in a mini jar or bowl of honey but accompanied by a little honey dipper, of course. Adding in a honey dipper creates an interactive component for your guests to enjoy. Word to the wise: Do not underestimate the power of honey. One time, my friends and I were enjoying a lovely wedge of gruyere and a friend paired a crostini with a crumble of gruyere and topped it with a drizzle of honey—and wow! Best believe that everyone's next bite had a drizzle of honey on it.

Roasted Garlic

For all the garlic lovers, roast fresh garlic (pg. 86) to add a savory, rich addition to any bite. Once the garlic has been roasted, it changes into a spreadable powerhouse of flavors.

Jams, Jellies, and Preserves

Place your favorite jam on the board to add a gorgeous pop of color and some sweetness. Jams and preserves can completely change the flavor profile of a bite.

Mustards

Mustard adds a tangy flavor, similar to vinegar. If you decide to go with a grainy mustard, you will get both flavor and texture.

Nuts

There is a wide variety of nut options. I typically go for a salted assortment to cover my bases. While making boards, I discovered a Brazil nut. I had never had it before, and now I love them. If you haven't tried one, be on the lookout. Nuts are commonly used as a salty crunch, but you can also use them for a sweet crunch with something like pecan pralines. (I always bring out pecan pralines during the winter holidays.)

5. Taste the Rainbow

After steps one through four, you will be left with pockets of space—some small and some big. I like to add in my fruits and veggies by size, starting with the biggest fruits (to ensure I have enough space) and ending with the smallest fruits. About 90 percent of the time, I gravitate to adding fruits instead of veggies.

Fruit gives your board color and a multitude of textures. Fruits, ideally, are juicy, crisp, and smooth, whereas vegetables have a limited color palette and tend to mostly fall into the crisp and robust texture category. Regardless of your preferences, in-season fruits and vegetables will guarantee freshness and high-quality flavor every time.

My frequent fruits include:

- Fresh citrus (clementines and blood oranges)

- Berries

- Grapes (I prefer red as opposed to green grapes. Red grapes tend to have a sweeter flavor profile than green grapes, which tend to be more tangy and sour.)

- Seasonal fruits (The board on p. 49 utilizes fresh figs, which are stunning, and slices of whole pomegranates. I recommend keeping the pomegranates in the peel so they are more accessible, and because the individual seeds are small so they can slip into the background.)

Tip: Slice your pomegranate at the last minute to ensure the flesh does not turn.

The go-to order for adding fruits is typically as follows: pears, pomegranates, grapes, strawberries, clementines, blackberries, raspberries, and blueberries.

Carbs

Don't worry, I didn't forget the crackers—nor have I ever forgotten the crackers. Who doesn't love carbs? I am not sure if you have noticed, but none of my boards have any bread, crackers, or any sort of bread or grain carb on the actual board itself. The reason for this can be attributed to my grandma Christine. When I started making boards, everyone I knew was eating charcuterie because I wanted to try and perfect my styling skills and get feedback. My grandma's one critique, which was so hard for her to tell me because she would never say anything bad, was that the crackers on her board became soggy. From that day forward, crackers were banned from my boards, and rule number four in my Thirteen Rules was solidified: "Save yourself the potential sogginess and place the crackers on the side."

Honesty, I have yet to find a way to place carbs on my board without moisture causing sogginess. No need to fret though—the carb board is here. This board has a variety of crackers with different textures, flavor profiles, and sizes. It is important to provide your guests with different types of crackers, so they can mix and match and find their favorite combinations. Another pro tip to having different styles and types of crackers is your ability to get an array of shapes to play around with the height, shapes, and colors.

Styling Tip: When garnishing your carbs or carb board, *beware of moisture*. To err on the side of caution, I try to stray away from using fresh flowers or fruits. For this board, using dried citrus, dried apricots, thyme, and lavender keeps your board vibrant and dry.

Shapes & Sizes for All

When selecting a board, it's important to consider a few factors:

1. Board Shape

Boards can be round, square, rectangular, and anything in between. Always consider how many people will be enjoying your board and ensure you have enough space to work with. A general rule of thumb is round boards create easy access to all items, and a round shape is open and all-inclusive. A square or rectangle shape creates more pockets and edges, which may feel more intimidating to a guest and may be harder for them to access. Each shape has its pros and cons, but it is important for you to try out different options and see what your preference is; and hey, your preference may change as you go through your creative charcuterie journey.

Tip: You do not always have to fill your board fully. Utilizing negative space to create contrast can help guide attention to certain focal points.

2. Board Color

Board colors can vary greatly depending on the material of the board. The color of the actual board you are working with sets the stage and vibe for the rest of the creative process. Think about your board as the canvas in an art project—if you start with a blue canvas, you will most likely not use blue paint because it will not show up well. The same concept applies to a board—if you have a dark-colored board you may want to highlight lighter colors that will pop instead of darker colors that may blend in. The table on the next page will dive deeper into common board colors and how best to style them.

Type	Overview	Example
Wooden Boards	Wooden boards are great for any and every occasion. When using a wooden board, the shade of wood used will greatly impact which colors of your charcuterie pop. For example, when using a lighter-colored wooden board, you want to focus on using darker foods like blackberries, cherries, tomatoes, and blueberries to create contrast. With a darker-colored wooden board, you'll want to do the opposite and focus on lighter-colored foods like raspberries, clementines, and cucumbers. **Pro Tip:** If you leave any sort of berry on your board, be careful it does not stain. If it stains, use water and baking soda to create a paste and leave it on your board overnight.	
Marble Boards	Marble boards are great when using dark colors because the light marble and the vibrant fruit and veggies create a stunning contrast.	
Slate Boards	The lighter the color of your food, the more it will pop on the dark-colored slate boards. Notice how the lighter colored foods like the golden berries and cucumber instantly pop, whereas the blackberries are subtle and provide a texture component as opposed to a color component.	

3. Board Design

Boards come in all sorts of designs. Each offers a unique set of pros and cons in terms of functionality, cohesiveness, and overall appearance. A functional board may be something with a handle to make transportation easy or edges to ensure the board is nice and secured. A cohesive board may be a certain size to be logical for the event you are hosting. Finally, an overall appearance board may be a board shaped to match a theme. The table below will highlight a few board design options.

Boards with handles	Boards with handles give the creator a more definitive canvas to work with because the center can easily be located based on the handle. Using a handled board makes transportation easy, too.	
Boards with edges	Boards with an edge around them are the easiest for transportation and creation. Think of your boards with edges like a bowling lane with the bumpers on. You can easily place food on the board without fear of spillage. An edge creates security for transportation since everything is nicely and neatly packed onto your board.	
Plates	Everyone has plates. Using a plate is a simple and fun twist on your idea of a standard charcuterie "board." In most cases a charcuterie plate is best for smaller size gatherings based on the sizes of plates. For example, a standard dinner plate would be a great serving size for two or three people.	
Unique shapes	Utilizing an unconventional board shape can help carry out a party theme or character focus. A theme or character can sometimes be difficult to incorporate on your average square board—make your life easier, treat yourself and use the board as your theme. A non-traditionally shaped board can be intimidating, but give yourself enough time, be prepared, have a plan, and give it a shot.	

4. Board Sizes

Serving size can be tricky because there are many factors to consider. I covered this topic thoroughly in the "Serving Size" section on pg. 31. When selecting a board, my go-to thought is, "Is this a main course or an appetizer?" Once that initial thought is addressed, I can begin the process of narrowing down the perfect board size. As we learned earlier in this section, boards come in various shapes and sizes; however, here is the guide I have come up with.

Board Size	Serving Size	Photo
Twelve-inch square	Three or four people	
Fourteen-inch round board	Four to eight people	
Twelve-by-sixteen-inch rectangle	Eight to twelve people	

You can create something unique and beautiful on almost anything you have. Do not be afraid to try different shapes, sizes, and colors of boards. Over time, you will begin to realize what type of board you prefer. I have become so accustomed to boards with edges, so when I don't have those bowling bumper lanes, I am in for a reality check. I take my edgeless boards as a challenge and work through it!

THE SCIENCE OF CHARCUTERIE

Creating charcuterie boards brought together my love for arts and crafts and food. While scrolling through Pinterest, I came across a photo of a color wheel. I started to analyze it and realized that, for the most part, I use every color on my boards. I then made the connection that a color directly across from another color was almost like the "opposite," and if you place those colors near one another on the color wheel, it creates a dramatic contrast. This was my *aha!* moment.

When I started my deep dive into charcuterie boards, I was always drawn to boards full of color and life and knew that was what I wanted to create. To me, colors can portray a message, and I realized my love for color and vibrance, as well as being over the top. I had to also realize that just because that is what I love does not mean it is what everyone else loves or wants all the time.

You first eat with your eyes, right? So, if a food is vibrant and full of color, it will be appealing and look enticing. I believe eating colorfully makes life more fun. We will get into the science shortly. This chapter simply aims to address the concept of colors.

The Senses

Our five main senses are touch, taste, vision, smell, and hearing. Each of these senses is housed in different parts of the brain and plays a role in the experience of eating. The first senses to be activated in terms of eating are smell, hearing, and sight. The perfect example of visualizing the connection between senses and food is Christmas morning. You wake up to the smell of freshly roasted coffee and sweet maple syrup. As you walk down the stairs, you begin to hear the sizzling and crackling of bacon, and then you hear *pop* and the toast is done.. As you grab your smooth porcelain plate and begin to serve the breakfast spread, you open the tin foil and are instantly attracted to the vegetable quiche because of its colors. Your eyes catch the vibrant colors from the fresh fruit, and you stack up pancakes and start to drizzle syrup. By this time, your plate is overflowing with your favorite classic breakfast foods and colorful fruit, sweet and salty aromas fill the air from the bacon and maple syrup. Now, it's time to taste it. Taste is the most self-explanatory of the senses, but let's just say Christmas breakfast almost always tastes good. As you begin to devour your plate, you fill your fork with all the different textures and tastes to curate your perfect bite.

There are many sensory opportunities when you look at a board; however, due to the nature of a board, the most impressionable is visual. Charcuterie boards are not necessarily aromatic, and they don't traditionally have auditory input like crackling bacon, which leaves the emphasis on the sense of sight. When you think about it, if something looks good, your brain will be inclined to perceive it as "tasting good." Thus, it is almost scientific that colorful and aesthetically pleasing food tastes better, so go forth and make a vibrant board full of color to entice your appetite.

If you still need convincing about the importance of capitalizing on the senses, let's dive into memory. Some memories, depending on a plethora of factors, are stronger or more memorable than others. These are often referred to as core memories. A factor that contributes to the strength or power of your memory is the sensations. Since the act of eating involves many of the senses, a memory established around eating is naturally a stronger memory.

Think back to the first time you ate your favorite food or splurged on a treat you rarely indulged in. When I think back, my favorite is a cinnamon roll from a little mom-and-pop shop on Main Street in Seal Beach, California. My papa has a vintage 1932 Ford, and he would often take it to car shows to show off while mingling with his fellow old dudes and talking about paint, engines, and tires. These discussions were over my head, especially as a kid, but why did I look forward to these car shows? For the cinnamon roll. The bakery was next to the shell shop, another frequent stop of mine. My family and I would stroll down Main Street, and suddenly, the smell of sweet, rich baked goods overpowered the smell of gasoline. As we walked closer, I could hear the screen door squeak as people walked out, and the rustling of filled paper bags as people anxiously waited to open their little Styrofoam box to reveal the best treat. When we opened the door, sensory overload hit in the best way possible. Through the glass shelves, my eyes darted from the brightly colored cookies and cakes to the double chocolate fudge brownies. As soon as my eyes caught that cinnamon roll, it was all over. The best part of the cinnamon roll was watching the worker drizzle the icing over the top. Once we made our way back outside, we would sit on the running board of the '32 and chow down. This cinnamon roll is so nostalgic and such a memory of joy and excitement. This is the type of memory you want to create when your family and friends have your board.

Characteristics of Food

We went over the senses, but let's get even deeper and look at the traits that make food good. Food is broken into three different characteristics: texture, flavor, and appearance.

Texture

Selfishly, texture is such an important factor for me. I love all types of texture and need my food to encompass texture to be enjoyable. I consider the main food textures to be chewy, creamy, crunchy, firm, and watery. When creating a board, you want to make sure you include as many textures as possible.

Here is a breakdown of what items I use to incorporate all the textures:

Chewy	Creamy	Crunchy	Firm	Watery
Salami	Sun Spread	Crostini	Semi-soft cheese	Clementines
Dried fruits	Brie	Cucumbers	(gouda, pepper	Honey
	Chevre	Carrots	jack, etc.)	Mustard
		Grapes	Strawberry	

Of course, many of these items are a "mixed consistency" or "mixed texture." For example, a strawberry could be considered firm; if it's a large ripe strawberry, it may also be considered juicy. Texture provides sensory input during the eating experience; naturally, if food has the intended texture, it indicates quality and freshness. For example, if you bite into a fresh cucumber and it's firm with a nice crunch, that indicates it is fresh and of good quality. Being thoughtful about the textures you incorporate on your board will be a game-changer in how your loved ones enjoy their board.

Flavor

Flavor is simply how something tastes. Typically, flavor is broken down into five categories: sweet, salty, umami, bitter, and sour. I do not necessarily want something bitter or sour, but others love it. To be nice, I strive to include a balance between every flavor, so there's something for everyone.

Umami is the fifth flavor category. Umami means "savory" in Japanese. Mushrooms, aged cheeses, and green tea are some foods that are in the umami flavor category.

Here is a list of foods I commonly use to hit each flavor profile:

Sweet	Salty	Umami	Bitter	Sour
Fruit	Cheese	Charcuterie	Arugula	Kumquats
Sweet and	Charcuterie	Mushrooms	Dill	Citrus
nutty chevre	Crackers	Aged cheeses	Blood oranges	Golden berries
Dried fruit		(parmesan, gouda,	Grapefruit	Green apples
		cheddar, etc.)		Balsamic glaze

Appearance

Appearance is made up of shape, size, and color. When making a board, it is important to include varying shapes of your food. Shapes can seem intimidating, but I will tell you a little secret: use a knife. You can use a knife to cut almost anything into a unique shape. Let's take the beloved strawberry, for example; you can create a zigzag shape, slice the strawberry into rounds, or slice it down the middle to create a triangle.

Size plays a role from the start. How big is the board? From there, what large items will your board contain? What small items will your board contain? As with anything, it is important to make sure your board has small and large items. Large and small items play an important part for your guests. Think about when you're creating a bite. You need the large item to serve as the vehicle for your bite or the star of your bite, and you need your small items to change the flavor or texture. Some of my favorite small items are different things like nuts, grapes, or cheese crumbles. My favorite larger items are brie, cucumber, and salami.

Next up is color. Color makes eating food vibrant and exciting. The next section will take you through details of color and the insane impact it can have on your board experience.

When making a board, do not forget to take a moment and think about texture, appearance, and flavor. With a little focus on these three areas, your board will be full of flavor and look almost too stunning to eat.

Color Wheel: Edible Edition

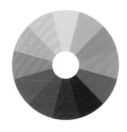

Let's start with the basics:

Primary Colors

The primary colors are red, blue, and yellow. These three colors cannot be created from other colors.

Secondary Colors

The secondary colors are green, orange, and violet. Secondary colors are created by mixing two primary colors on opposing sides of the color wheel.

Tertiary Colors

There are six tertiary colors. When you mix a primary color with a secondary color, you make a tertiary color.

Color Contrast Pairs Chart:

Every color will have another color with which it creates the most contrast. Color contrast happens when colors are directly opposed on the color wheel. For example, red's highest contrast color is green because it is directly opposite it on the color wheel. Red's lowest contrast colors are purple and orange because they are directly next to red on the color wheel.

What does a color wheel have to do with charcuterie boards? Well, funny you ask—placing a strawberry next to a cucumber creates a high color contrast that allows the strawberry and cucumber to each pop and stand out. If you place the strawberry next to a clementine, there will be low color contrast, which, to the eye, does not create that "look at me" effect because the clementine and strawberry are next to like colors.

The table below will dive into each color of the rainbow, a food that is that color, and a visual of what will create the highest contrast versus the lowest color contrast.

Color	Food	Create the *most* color contrast	Create the *least* color contrast
Red	Strawberries Pomegranates		
Orange	Clementines		
Yellow	Pineapple Honey		
Green	Cucumbers Grapes		
Blue	Blueberries		
Purple	Blackberries Grapes		
Pink	Salami Prosciutto Raspberries		
White	Asiago Irish cheddar Boursin		

Charcuterie Compare & Contrast

Both boards have essentially the same items on them, so why do they look so different?

At their core, these boards are similar. They both have a salami river, a cucumber river, and a brie river. They also have honey, basil spread, sweet and nutty chevre, and spicy herb goat cheese. Both boards have the same assortment of fruit and crudités, yet they do not look like twins. They don't even look like sisters. Cousins maybe?

The main reason for this is because of the placement of the **colors.**

Rectangle Board

The rectangle board has major contrast going on. Almost every item on this board is strategically placed next to an item that provides the greatest contrast. For example, the raspberries next to the blueberries, and the strawberries next to the blackberries. Placing the green basil spread next to the rich, purple grapes lets both items pop. Let's take a closer look at the garnish: using pale pink chrysanthemums in conjunction with beautiful goldenrod flowers also creates a noticeable contrast that allows us to appreciate the beauty of both.

Round Board

The round board has minimal contrast going on. All the fruits are strategically placed next to fruits with similar colors. For example, the blueberries are next to the blackberries. The main garnish on this board is dried fruit, dried citrus, rosemary, and dill. Both dried fruit and citrus offer a pop of muted color. The rosemary and dill serve the purpose of adding texture rather than a pop of color. The lavender's prominent sage green accents served as an understated color variation, but they aren't overpowering.

Color contrast is something to consider and focus on because it truly sets the mood for the event. For example, if you are going for a neutral aesthetic, a board with minimal color contrast is the way to go. If you are going for a springtime floral aesthetic, a board with higher color contrast will be the way to go. Both desired aesthetic and your preferences should be kept in mind. High contrast, bright boards are clearly my forte; however, they are not everyone's cup of tea, which is okay. My goal is to make sure you have the knowledge and skills to make low- and high-contrast boards.

GARNISH: SHE IS BEAUTY, SHE IS GRACE

I have always loved accessorizing. I wore uniforms for almost all my childhood. Whether it was my school uniform or my soccer uniform, I did not have the opportunity to express myself with my clothing. To be honest, looking at old pictures, maybe that was for the best—just kidding. Anyway, because I had so few ways to express myself, ever since I can remember I always painted my nails and wore jewelry. I have a ring made from a spoon passed down from my great-granny that I have worn forever. I love the idea of constantly wearing these accessories because it adds to any outfit and feels like a part of who I am. When looking at me, based on my excessive rings, necklaces, and bracelets, it's no surprise that my boards are also highly "accessorized." I look at accessories the same way I look at garnishes. Garnishes are small details that have the potential to add so much. The most simplistic board can be elevated to simple and chic with a few intentional additions.

When I started creating boards, I realized adding garnish was one of my favorite parts of the process. It all started because I was fortunate to have access to the basics right in my backyard: citrus, lavender, and rosemary. As I played around with color combinations, different herbs, and flowers, I learned what I liked best. I fell in love with the idea that a few flowers, herbs, and citrus could completely transform a board's vibe and color scheme. Garnishing is a time-consuming process that is a labor of love. When I make my plan, I like to allot about twenty to thirty minutes for garnishing.

Dried Citrus

Dried citrus is a versatile accent to add to your board, tablescape, packaging, and more. Citrus is a budget-conscious, sustainable, and easy way to add color, texture, and a unique personal touch to your creations.

I am fortunate to have an abundance of citrus at my disposal—not only in my backyard but in my neighbors', who graciously let me hijack their citrus anytime. Having dried citrus on hand has become routine for me, and I have found many useful ways to incorporate it on boards and with many other options.

Adding a little dried citrus and herb to a gift bag is a nice personal touch. I use dried citrus to garnish wrapped boards and cracker bags. I have even seen some people keep the citrus around the house for cleaning and adding fragrance, which I love to see and smell.

You can also always use fresh or dried citrus to make a vibrant tablescape. Here is a tablescape I created with citrus and eucalyptus for a bridal shower. In October 2021, one of my good friends (my big sister from my sorority days) got married and asked me to be a bridesmaid. This was the first wedding I was in, and it was such a special and meaningful experience to share with her. If you know my big sis (a.k.a. the bride), she has always been the epitome of class and chic, so naturally, using dried citrus, lavender, and eucalyptus was the perfect way to go.

Tablescape: a table setting involving decorative accents like flowers, candles, place settings, greenery, etc., used for social events, dinners, etc.

I love to use citrus on my boards, accompanied by fresh fruit and flowers. Dried citrus is also a fantastic way to garnish your carb boards because there is no moisture, so everything stays nice and crisp.

Dried Citrus Recipe

This recipe's only ingredient is citrus. The serving size will depend on the amount of citrus you choose to use (e.g., one orange or ten).

1. Slice your favorite citrus into quarter-inch-thick slices. My favorite types of citrus to use are lemons, limes, and blood oranges.

2. Place citrus slices on a wire rack on top of a sheet pan.

3. Place in oven for 7–8 hours at 250°F (121°C).

4. Let them cool, and you are ready to garnish your boards and tablescapes!

Herbs

The first garnish I used regularly was herbs. Luckily, I was able to take advantage of my garden and my neighbors' gardens to harvest rosemary and oregano. These two herbs were the catalyst for my love of garnishing. Most boards, unfortunately, do not offer a strong aromatic component simply due to the nature of the foods, but you are in luck because most herbs have strong aromas. I think if I had to choose between using herbs or florals for the rest of my life, my heart says florals because of the colors, but my brain says herbs because they are so multipurpose. Herbs can be used purely as garnish, and since green is not widely used in boards (only with cucumbers or green grapes), the green herb is almost always guaranteed to pop. Not only is it a garnish, but it also adds flavor. I like to use herbs as much as possible, and I always use them to marinate mozzarella or for my spicy herb chevre. I strive to use fresh herbs mostly, but that doesn't always happen; dried herbs are also good for cooking purposes. My favorite herbs to use right now are rosemary and dill.

Depending on your weather, you can try to grow some herbs. The convenience of having fresh herbs at your disposal is like no other. If you are in a pinch and have a recipe needing a nice little punch, hit it with some fresh rosemary.

If you do not have a green thumb or live in an herb-unfriendly climate, I recommend storing your herbs stem-side down in a jar of water and covering the top of the plant with a plastic bag. Refresh the water periodically to make sure the herb is living its best life.

This table provides a full breakdown of the different herbs that I most commonly use as well as their flavor profile.

	Herb	Flavor Profile
	Rosemary	Rosemary is strong and potent. Rosemary's texture is thick, and it packs a lot of flavor. Rosemary as a garnish can minorly affect the flavors of the surrounding food. I love using rosemary—just do so with caution and care.
	Dill	Dill is a fresh and light herb with citrusy undertones. Dill has a beautiful, rich, dark-green color that adds a pop to any board.
	Thyme	Thyme is a mild herb with peppery undertones. Thyme makes for a great garnish because it is dainty and delicate. It has a wooden-like stem, which adds great color variation.
	Basil	Basil has a complex flavor profile because it can be both sweet and savory. Basil is extremely aromatic and has a vibrant light green color to brighten your boards.
	Sage	Sage has a distinct earthy flavor and goes well with strongly flavored dishes. Sage is an understated, mute-green color with gray undertones. This herb is also extremely delicate. My favorite time of year to use sage as a garnish is Christmas and New Year's.
	Oregano	Oregano has a mild bitter flavor with earthy undertones. This herb makes for a great garnish because of its unique ivy-colored green shade and tiny, intricate leaves.

Flowers

My mom has always naturally had a green thumb, so the backyard is always full of beautiful flowers and greens. When I started making boards, I took full advantage of the garden. My first boards prominently featured oregano, rosemary, and lavender. As I started researching flowers and creating my inventory of food-safe edible flowers, I expanded the types I used and liked. Not all the flowers I have tried taste good, so when someone inevitably holds up a little chamomile flower and asks, "Can I eat this?" I say, "Yes, but I would not," and leave it at that.

I often receive questions about edible flowers and how I know which ones are safe. Unfortunately, my answer is, genuinely, through research. Flowers are more complicated than I could have ever imagined because there are different strands and species, and they have long complicated scientific names. With many internet searches, I have curated a list of my most utilized and food-safe flowers.

My favorite flowers to use are lavender, nasturtiums, chamomile, marigolds, pansies, and chrysanthemums.

The table provides you with a description of the flowers I gravitate toward. The flowers in the table are edible; however, I do not recommend eating them because I find them to be extremely bitter—but give them a try. The main function of using flowers on my boards is to add dimension, texture, and, of course, color.

Flowers	Look	Description
Lavender		Lavender is something that can be easily grown and maintained. It adds a beautiful minor fragrance to the board. There are many different types of lavender, but for the most part, they have a muted pastel tone that pops against your cucumber river or brie wheel.
Chamomile		The bright yellow center of the chamomile in contrast with the little white petals adds such a small but mighty pop of color. When styling these flowers, if you want the flower to lie flat on top of brie, make sure you cut the stem as close to the base as possible. If you place the flower in something like strawberries or grapes, keep the stem a little longer to increase stability.
Marigold		Marigolds have multiple layers of petals that, by nature, make them thicker flowers with a larger sturdy stem. Due to the stem, it's important to focus on the placement of the flower because it needs to be supported to remain in place.

Pansies		Pansies are extremely delicate flowers with beautifully colored petals. They are versatile since they have a small stem and can lie flat. These flowers are extremely delicate, so please handle with care. **Style Tip:** If you have pansies that have fallen apart, do not throw them away! Save them and use the petals to cover a log of plain goat cheese or decorate brie.
Chrysanthemum (mums)		Chrysanthemums, or mums for short, are one of the most versatile and colorful flowers you can add to a board. These flowers can range greatly in size and color. They are sturdy, making them optimal for placement throughout a board. Mums can be large, which can be overpowering, so if you feel like using a large mum, be aware of its placement. Typically, when using bigger flowers, I like to place them on the outskirts of the board instead of the center.

Roses Are...Delicious

Placing a rose to an empty space is a delicious functional addition to any board. I love the look of a cucumber rose, especially on a veggie board.

> **Tip:** Use a small 2 oz plastic cup to keep your cucumber rose in place. Use toothpicks to keep your salami rose petals intact.

When creating a rose, I consider two main tactics. The first method involves some insane knife skills or using a mandolin. For a rose made of vegetable, like a cucumber or watermelon radish, focus on creating thin and equal slices. The slices should be bendable and able to be manipulated to form perfect rose petals—or should I say cucumber petals. The second method is for charcuterie, like salami. You want to have some toothpicks at the ready, and you'll start by laying out four pieces and folding them in half. Once they are all folded in half and lined up, start at one end and roll them as tightly as possible. From there, you can add in more folded pieces until your rose reaches your desired size.

Roasted Garlic

During my undergraduate years, one of my roommates decided to slice the top of a head of garlic, drizzle some olive oil on it, and toss it in the oven. Let me tell you, my garlic-loving self was mind blown! Once the garlic is perfectly roasted, you give it a gentle squeeze, and the garlic oozes out into a perfect spreadable texture. I am content toasting a piece of sourdough and lathering it up with a few cloves of roasted garlic. But then I thought, *What a fun and interactive addition this would be to a charcuterie board.*

If the board were exclusively for me, the focus would be garlic. Unfortunately, the average human does not want to be warding vampires off as much as I do. In fact, my mom has mixed feelings about garlic, which is a tragedy in my eyes, but to each their own. Supposedly, when my mom was pregnant with me, my dad decided to be the in-home chef. He roasted a full pound of garlic and stored it in the fridge, which caused everything to taste and smell like garlic. Ever since, my mom has been anti-garlic, but I have not let that stop me.

The concept of adding roasted garlic to your board allows each person to make their own choice as to whether they are going to be a garlic lover or hang with the vampires. Don't forget, a simple squeeze and the roasted garlic will come right out. It packs a powerful punch and adds to any charcuterie combination or even your favorite sourdough toast.

When using roasted garlic as a garnish, I like to add it near or on top of my savory spreads like sun spread, spicy herb chevre, or soft gouda cheese. Since garlic is not everyone's cup of tea, I like to keep it near the edge of the board with flavor profiles that complement the garlic nicely.

ROASTED GARLIC RECIPE

Ingredients

Your desired amount of whole garlic (I tend to use 3–8 bulbs of garlic)

Salt

Pepper

Olive oil

Serving Size

Up to you; however, I typically add 1–2 bulbs per board.

Directions

1. Slice off the top of the garlic.

2. Place garlic in tin foil.

3. Add a pinch of salt and pepper on top.

4. Drizzle with olive oil.

5. Cover the top of the garlic with tin foil.

6. Place in oven for 20–25 minutes at 200°F (93°C).

Fruit Garnish

The fruit garnish came to be when I received an odd request for no flowers or herbs on a board. I was perplexed, to say the least. Of course, I took this as a personal challenge, so the fruit garnish was born. As a flower child, I cannot resist and still use flowers with fruit garnish. The flower garnish is utilized independently and in conjunction with other garnishes to maximize color and add a touch of fun. Often when I create smaller boards, I have a tough time fitting in larger fruits like strawberries or fresh figs, so the fruit garnish is an ingenious way to add color and get in another fruit or two.

To incorporate a fruit garnish:

1. Start with a larger fruit, like a slice of a strawberry or a dried apricot.

2. Time to slice. Slicing your fruit in half widens the color palette of your board and adds dimension. Look at that blackberry!

3. From there, you will want to place your halved medium fruit on opposing sides of your large fruit.

4. Add in the little guys, like blueberries, golden berries, or kumquats.

5. The final step, as always, is flower power!

Styling Tip: When using fruit to garnish, you can get the most bang for your buck by making one simple slice. What do I mean by this? Well, on the outside, a blackberry is dark purple; however, once you slice it, it reveals a beautiful, rich, pink center with a white outline and then a dark purple outline. By slicing open the blackberry to intentionally use it as garnish, you have gained three different colors that all complement and contrast one another well.

Brie'tiful

I like to believe every charcuterie lover has that one cheese that made them fall in love and obsess over making a board, just so they can use that *one* cheese. That one cheese for me was brie. When I first started creating boards, brie was a treat because it was not something I regularly had on hand or had any reason to buy. Even as I became more exposed to the abundance of cheese selections, I continued to gravitate toward my first love, brie. I love brie because it has so many different textures, and due to its mildness, it pairs well with just about anything.

Brie will always have a special place in my heart. It is a versatile cheese for styling, due to its sturdy rind and soft creamy insides. The sturdy rind allows designs to hold up and be prominent. The soft, creamy inside lets you "jam-pack" (literally and figuratively) the brie with anything your cheesy heart desires.

Filled Brie

1. When removing the brie from the fridge, make sure it is nice and chilled.

2. Use a cookie cutter of your choice. I frequently use a circle cookie cutter, as it is reliable and simple. It creates a simple canvas for implementing multiple different designs.

3. Center the cookie cutter, and slowly apply even pressure to push the cookie cutter to the other side of the brie.

4. Carefully remove the cookie cutter and the inside of the brie.

Tip: Save the round brie inside for another board.

5. Place your brie in its desired location on the board.

6. Start by adding dried apples, apricots, and raisins. They will help contain and manage any moisture.

7. Layer in the fresh fruits of your choice.

8. Top with a honeycomb, pops of color, and, of course, garnish.

The Glitz & Glam

Feelin' bougie? Just add glitter—edible glitter, of course! I needed something to add a *wow* factor to my boards and emphasize key details like a twenty-first birthday or anniversary date. I have used edible glitter in many ways. Using cutouts, I added "21" for a birthday and wanted a pop; glitter was exactly what the board needed. Channeling my sustainable self, I used cookie cutouts to create numbers and then add some glitter. Edible glitter is so fun and adds an extra special touch that truly elevates your board. To ensure maximum shimmer, wait until it's time to serve before adding glittering touches to your board.

Edible glitter is typically made of sugar, cornstarch, and color additives. To be safe, always check the ingredients and do your research to ensure that all items are edible.

SEMI-HOMEMADE
SHOWSTOPPERS

I watched many cooking shows growing up and found myself always gravitating toward the shows that made food simple and realistic. Cooking can be so intimidating, which causes stress and frustration. I find that when a portion of the recipe is from a mix or store-bought, I feel a weight lifted off my shoulders. In my book, semi-homemade is not cheating. This chapter focuses on creating beautiful and simple dishes that can be served alone and in conjunction with a charcuterie board. Semi-homemade recipes are the best way to go because they give you a solid and reliable foundation while allowing you the opportunity to be creative. I am a true believer and live by the motto, "Work smarter, not harder," which is the backbone of this chapter. If you don't tell anyone, no one will know you're cutting corners. Your secret is safe with me.

BRIE & BLACKBERRY TART

Ingredients

Wedge of your favorite brie (I used
    triple creamed)
Approximately 25 blackberries
Pie crust
One egg yolk

Serving Size

4-6 people

Pro Tip: Grab a bowl
smaller than your pie crust,
place it in the middle,
outline the bowl, and voilà!
You have a perfect circle
to work in.

My name is Melissa, and I use store-bought crust. Do not get me wrong, I have gone through the process and put in the work to make homemade dough, but it is not my forte and that is okay because store-bought dough was made for a reason. The beautiful brie and blackberry tart is indeed made on store-bought crust. If you are a homemade dough enthusiast, be my guest and make your own. However, if you are not talented in that area—off to the grocery store you go! This recipe came to be because the store-bought dough came with two pie crusts. I opened the fridge and found some blackberries and got to brainstorming. Brie is almost always on hand in my house because it is simply perfect whenever you're craving something rich and creamy.

Directions

1. Lay out your pie crust.

2. Slice your brie into thin strips—about a quarter of an inch thick. You will want to make sure all slices are a uniform thickness to the best of your ability, so each piece melts at the same rate.

3. Arrange your brie evenly around the pie crust. The entire crust does not need to be covered in brie because it will melt.

4. Next, grab your blackberries. I arrange mine in each quadrant of the circle. Do not use all the blackberries because you will need to use some as garnish.

5. Using your drawn circle as a guide, fold over the excess outer dough to create a nice edge.

6. Separate the whites of your egg from the yolk (save your egg whites for your next scrambled egg), beat your egg yolk, and brush on an even egg wash.

7. Bake your brie at 350°F (176°C) and check in at 20 minutes. If it is not a stunning golden brown, check back in at the 25-minute mark.

8. Garnish with your remaining fresh berries. I like to slice a few of my blackberries open, adding some more natural colors.

9. For the remaining garnish, I use dried citrus, rosemary, and lavender.

BURRATA & HEIRLOOM TOMATO SALAD

Ingredients

5–6 medium heirloom tomatoes (try to grab some tomatoes with varying colors like red, yellow, etc.)

3–5 cherry tomatoes

½ cup (108 grams) of olive oil

Juice of ½ a medium-sized lemon

6–7 medium to large fresh basil leaves

8 oz (227 grams) burrata

Salt and pepper to taste

Balsamic glaze to taste

1–2 bulbs of roasted garlic

Serving Size

3–5 people

I have always been a tomato lover. In fact, my great-grandma, Granny, whom I have been told I am insanely similar to, used to eat sliced tomatoes with a sprinkle of salt and pepper to taste. Granny used to think BBQ chips were spicy, so it is safe to imply that she was taking it easy on the pepper. Anyway, one day, when I was little, I asked my mom if I could please have some sliced tomatoes. Weird, right? Ever since that day, I have loved tomatoes. This recipe was prepared for one of my first picnics and wine tastings. One of my good friends is a vegetarian, so I was brainstorming different ways to make vegetarian-friendly foods, and this recipe was born. Burrata is one of those cheeses that truly is a star and does not need much at all to be a showstopper. Burrata is a cow's milk cheese with a mozzarella-like exterior, but once you slice into it, the center is so rich yet simple, with a creamy texture. Since burrata is a showstopper, heirloom tomatoes make the perfect accent to this amazing cheese.

Directions

1. Slice your heirloom tomatoes into quarter-inch-thick rounds.

2. Place your tomatoes in alternating colors around the plate.

3. Once the tomatoes are placed to your liking, season with a mixture of half olive oil and half lemon juice, and add salt and pepper to taste.

4. Add in fresh basil.

5. Gently place burrata in the center of the plate. Burrata's soft center requires tender love and care when handling it.

6. Slice cherry tomatoes into rounds to fill in the gaps and add a different texture.

7. Garnish with roasted garlic (pg. 86) and fresh flowers (pg. 80).

8. Finally, top the burrata with a nice swirl of balsamic glaze. The swirl is a personal style choice, not a necessity.

9. Serve with crostini (pg. 116) and/or your favorite crunchy cracker. I recommend serving this dish with something that adds a nice crunch. A crunchy cracker will give the bite some texture to offset the soft burrata and dense tomatoes.

WHITE WINE & THYME-GRILLED BRIE

Ingredients

22 oz (624 grams) of brie (preferably in a wheel shape)

4–5 springs of fresh thyme

½ cup (113 grams) of white wine

Serving Size

6–10 people

This recipe was a complete experiment that turned out to be a winner. I wish I could take the credit for it, but Kfran (a.k.a. the grill master, a.k.a. my dad) had this idea, and I added my own flair. Baked brie is always delicious, but it can be hard to make it appeal aesthetically to our visual senses. Brie has a creamy soft inside that is the definition of ooey-gooey once it hits the right temperature. Unfortunately, ooey-gooey is delicious but not always pretty. Grilling the brie makes the middle ooey-gooey but crisps the rind just enough, so it holds its shape and keeps that ooey-gooey goodness contained. This grilled recipe was such a yummy addition to my dinner.

Directions

1. Slice about ½ an inch off the top of your brie to remove the rind from the top to expose the creamy inside. By removing the rind only from top, it ensures you will achieve the delicious-looking ooey-gooey bubbling.

2. Next, add your brie to a cast iron skillet. I know cast iron skillets are intimidating—I am still intimidated—but cast iron works best and makes you look like the confident chef you are!

3. Sprinkle fresh thyme on top of your brie. There is not a magic measurement for this; I use about 3–5 sprigs of thyme.

4. Open your wine. First thing's first, pour yourself a glass because I am sure you deserve it. Make sure there is enough remaining to cover your brie. Pour the wine over the top of the brie so the top has a nice layer, but only fill your cast iron up about halfway with wine.

5. Place brie on the grill at 550°F (288°C) for about 15 minutes.

6. Check on the brie periodically, about every 5 minutes, to ensure it does not burn. Once the insides start to bubble and you see the ooey-gooey start to happen, you'll know it's ready.

7. Carefully remove your cast iron from the grill and place it on something heat-resistant, like a trivet (I use trivets all the time but recently learned that name of them; maybe you just did, too).

8. Serve with your favorite fruits; I used fresh grapes. Add honey or jam, and, of course, do not forget the crostini (pg. 116).

SUMMERTIME CAPRESE

Ingredients

½ of a medium-sized watermelon
(refer to pg. 43 to find the best
watermelon)

2–3 medium-sized peaches

16 oz (454 grams) fresh mozzarella

14–16 medium fresh basil leaves

Balsamic glaze to taste

Serving Size

3–5 people

When I think of summer, I think of eating fresh juicy fruits while trying to get my tan on in the sun, slathered in sunscreen, of course. Once I became more confident with trying flavors, I started to develop a summer version of a classic caprese salad. As I sat in the sun munching on some watermelon, it came to me—summertime caprese salad. The sweet watermelon adds a firm crunch, perfectly offset by the saltiness of the mozzarella and the slightest bitterness from the peaches. The basil not only adds beautiful vibrance but gives the dish an aromatic factor and peppery kick. Finally, to finish off the already outstanding bite, the balsamic vinaigrette comes in and gives your palate a tangy sweet punch. The salad is the perfect addition to your next summertime BBQ or when you need a sophisticated snack.

Directions

1. Start by slicing your peach into rounds instead of quarters to create the most surface area. When you get to the pit, try to cut it out.

2. Next, use a circle cutter to create perfect watermelon rounds. If I have not convinced you to get a circle cutter, you can go freehand with a knife to make circles.

3. If your mozzarella is in a log or ball, it is time to slice it into rounds. Focus on creating the optimal amount of surface area.

4. Time to layer! Add a slice of fresh mozzarella, peaches, watermelon, and so on until your board is covered.

5. The basil garnish is next. Place fresh basil where you see fit. My rule of thumb is to always imagine each serving having a basil leaf. A serving for this dish would be a nice, neat stack of mozzarella, peach, watermelon, and basil.

6. Get your drizzle on! Top off your summer caprese with a drizzle of balsamic glaze. There is no right or wrong amount—I find it delicious, so I always add more, but it is up to your discretion.

7. Add your flower power! Since the summertime caprese is already flourishing with tons of color, I went with a simple and classic lavender garnish to add some purple.

Fun & Festive Skewers

Skewers have recently become one of my new favorite additions to boards, especially if it is for a party. Having skewers on a board or as a separate appetizer is a delicious and accessible item for your guests. The skewers started as the classic caprese skewer with mozzarella, tomatoes, and basil. Then I thought, *Hmm, why not add a little bit of fun?* I developed a few different skewers truly perfect for any season or occasion. With these skewers, you truly have the creative freedom to customize everything to your liking. I always stick to the classics, incorporating mozzarella and basil. You can never go wrong with a classic!

This table compiles my favorite skewers for any occasion. Each skewer has a twist on a classic caprese salad skewer and makes the perfect addition to any charcuterie board, but also works as a stand-alone appetizer.

Skewer	Photo	Ingredients
Anytime		Marinate fresh mozzarella pearls in chili flakes, thyme, rosemary, basil, lemon zest, dill, and pepper, all to taste. On your skewer: Mozzarella Tomato Baby bell pepper Green olives Artichoke hearts Black olives Garnish with whatever fits your occasion. For these skewers, I used endives, nasturtiums, lavender, chamomile, and goldenrods.

Summer skewer		With a melon-baller, create perfect little balls using your favorite seasonal melons. I love to use cantaloupe, honeydew, and watermelon because they are delicious, and that color palette is perfection. Alternate a piece of melon, fresh and folded salami, and a fresh mozzarella ball. Garnish with fresh mint and lavender.
Holiday skewer		Marinate fresh mozzarella pearls in chili flakes, thyme, rosemary, basil, and pepper, all to taste. On your skewer: Green olive Tomato Marinated mozzarella Fresh basil Black olive Garnish with fresh rosemary to keep your color palette in the holiday spirit. **Styling Tip:** Place a round bowl in the middle of your board while placing your skewers, then remove when everything is placed to get a perfect circle.

RECIPES: DON'T BE BOARD

When guests come over to my home for dinner or an event, there is usually a request tied to their RSVP: "Yes, we can come. Will you make [fill in the blank with their favorite recipe]?" I thought long and hard about what the most common *fill in the blank with their favorite recipe* recipes are. I decided my goal for this chapter is to compile the "classic" dishes created by my family and friends.

Every recipe that made the cut has been carefully selected and has a special place in my heart. By now, I am sure you have realized that my family and friends are something I cherish and value, so I wanted to include a special recipe from some of my favorite people, as well as some Boards by Melfran classics. One of the best things about these recipes is that they can be served with a board or on their own. Try them out and find your favorites.

Recipe Symbol Guide

	How long this item will stay fresh
	Styling suggestions and recommendations
	Tips and tricks to ensure success

SUN SPREAD

Sun spread is a Boards by Melfran original recipe with its vibrant color and delicious sun-dried tomato flavor. Upon its birth, it became a staple and fan favorite on every board I created. Pair this spread with crostini and fresh crudités, like cucumber. Sun spread is a definite must on your next board.

Ingredients

8 oz (227 grams) cream cheese, softened

½ cup (115 grams) mayo

½ cup (120 grams) sour cream

13 dashes of hot sauce (e.g., Crystal)

1 cup (54 grams) sun-dried tomatoes

½ cup (6 grams) chopped green onions

Salt and pepper to taste

Serving Size

4–5 people

Directions

1. Place all ingredients in a food processor.

2. Blend ingredients until smooth.

3. Place in the fridge overnight.

4. Serve with your favorite crackers or use as a pasta sauce.

 Pro Tip: If there happens to be any left (which I highly doubt), try it out over your favorite pasta noodles as a sauce.

 For pasta sauce, add in pasta water until you have reached your desired sauce consistency.

BASIL & WHITE BEAN SPREAD

Ingredients

15 oz (426 grams) cannellini white
    beans

1 tablespoon minced garlic

1 cup (20 grams) chopped fresh basil

Salt and pepper to taste

Serving Size

4–5 people

As my family and friends have gotten older and overall more health conscious, I knew there was a need for a vegan spread. My goal was to make a spread even non-vegans would want to eat. Lo and behold, the basil spread was made. **Warning:** Your home will smell of deliciously fresh basil for a few minutes, so live it up while you can. I love to toast fresh naan or pita bread, add the spread, and top with a crisp cucumber or radish.

Pro Tip: Squeeze fresh lemon on top to keep the vibrant green color alive.

Directions

1. Place all ingredients in a bowl.

2. Use an immersion blender to blend until smooth and spread becomes a beautiful green color.

3. Place in fridge to set for 24 hours.

4. Serve with warm pita as a dairy-free option on your board.

GRANDMA'S SEVEN-LAYER DIP

Ingredients

8 oz (227 grams) cream cheese

¾ cup (172 grams) mayonnaise

2 medium tomatoes

1 green pepper

2 green onions

1 green bell pepper

1 medium white onion

8 oz (227 grams) grated cheddar
   cheese

8 oz (227 grams) grated mozzarella
   cheese

Serving Size

8–12 people

Grandma Stien was born and raised in India until moving to Toronto, Canada, and finally to California. When my mom made her way to Toronto for the first time to meet her in-laws, she started going through major Mexican food withdrawals after a few days. At that time, trying to find Mexican food in Canada was almost impossible. My mom said when they arrived at the final family party of the day, a seven-layer dip was there. This dip was the only Mexican food she'd had in what felt like a year and she devoured it. Grandma Stien has her iconic, traditional Indian dishes, and American dishes with her Indian flair, and she also has her seven-layer dip. Attempting to gather a recipe from this woman was a challenge; everything is a "dash of this," "some of that," and all based on her intuition. With some help, love, and adaptation, here is the recipe for Grandma Stien's seven-layer dip.

Directions

1. Add 8 oz of room-temperature cream cheese and ¾ cup mayonnaise to a food processor and blend until combined.

2. Sharpen your knife and dice the following into bite-size chunks:

   > 2 medium tomatoes
   >
   > 1 green pepper
   >
   > 2 green onions
   >
   > 1 green bell pepper
   >
   > 1 medium white onion

3. In a medium-size clear glass dish, layer the following:

   > Cream cheese and mayonnaise mixture
   >
   > Jar of your favorite salsa (I recommend a chunkier salsa)
   >
   > Diced green peppers
   >
   > White onion
   >
   > Tomato
   >
   > Green onion

4. Top with grated cheddar and mozzarella cheese.

5. Garnish with a thinly sliced avocado by creating a diagonal row, alternating the orientation of the slices.

6. Add color with sliced bell pepper rounds.

7. Lastly, top with a hearty handful of cilantro. Let chill in the refrigerator for 1–2 hours before serving.

NANA'S DRESSING

Ingredients

Four 1.6 oz (45.5 grams) ranch
    seasoning packets
32 oz (907 grams) buttermilk
10.6 oz (300.5 grams) plain Greek
    yogurt (non-fat or 2 percent)
3 heaping tablespoons (44 grams)
    mayonnaise

Serving Size

4-6 medium to large salads

My nana is the type of home cook with a handful of items she prepares perfectly, one being her salad dressing. I must admit this salad dressing has made me a true ranch snob. Ranch in a bottle? No way. Growing up, my cousins and I put this dressing on everything, even pasta. These days, Nana's dressing is the staple dressing for salads at my house and any family gathering; if it's not Nana's, I don't want it. When my family is hosting, any veteran attendee expects to have Nana's salad dressing. Our go-to salad with Nana's dressing is romaine lettuce, shredded carrots, chopped purple cabbage, and croutons—the salad is so simple because the dressing is just that good. My mom occasionally tries to switch it up and use her Italian dressing, and let's just say it leaves some unhappy herbivores crunching on a sad salad.

Directions

1. Add buttermilk to the bowl.
2. Whisk in the 4 packets of ranch seasoning until combined.
3. Add 10.6 oz of Greek yogurt.
4. Add mayonnaise.
5. Stir until all ingredients until combined.
6. Place in the fridge for a minimum of 15 minutes. (Nana said she likes to make it at least a day in advance, so the flavors will set in.)

CROSTINI

Pro Tip: Slice your leftover crostini, add them to a bowl of your favorite greens, and top with Nana's dressing—magic!

Who doesn't love a crunchy, garlicky crostini as the vehicle for your favorite cheese? When I started creating boards, I played around with a plethora of crostini recipes to finally curate the best crostini. The entire house smells like the most delicious garlicky goodness, and my family gathers around to inform me that "this bread is too burned," to which I replied, "I will take care of it." If my sarcasm did not transfer well, the bread is not burnt. My beloved neighbors, who let me hijack their citrus, love my crostini. Every time I have any extra, once they cool, I pack them into a little bag, put them in their mailbox, and send a text: "Crostini in the mailbox!" I can safely assume that text message makes their evenings. My neighbors have said they are the perfect crouton for their Caesar salad.

Directions

1. Find the freshest French baguette possible.

2. Preheat the oven to 375°F (190°C). While your oven is preheating, make your garlic butter oil: In a bowl, add ½ stick of melted butter, ½ cup of olive oil, and desired amount of garlic (I am a garlic girl, so I add about 2 tablespoons).

3. Slice bread into rounds, about a quarter of an inch in thickness.

4. Brush your garlic butter oil onto both sides of your crostini round.

5. Place brushed crostini on a baking sheet.

6. Place your baking sheet into the oven for 20–25 minutes.

SHARON'S CHEESY GARLIC BREAD

Ingredients

1 loaf French bread (454 grams)

½ cup (113 grams) butter, softened

2 tablespoons (8 grams) fresh chopped parsley, divided

5 cloves minced garlic

1 cup (225 grams) fresh grated mozzarella cheese

½ cup (112.5 grams) fresh grated sharp cheddar cheese

½ cup (112.5 grams) fresh grated parmesan cheese

Serving Size

4-6 people

Sharon was my neighbor, whom I mentioned previously. She and her husband, Art, were my neighbors for as long as I can remember. I still own the handmade crochet quilt she gifted me when I was born. Sharon unfortunately passed away in 2021 and left behind many loved ones, as well as her recipes. Every Christmas, Art and Sharon would give my brother and me a chocolate advent calendar and her famous homemade cookies. Sharon also had delicious wontons. These wontons were something else, let me tell you! I received a text in my family group chat, "Sharon made wontons," and I drove forty-five miles home from Cal Poly Pomona to get my hands on them. They were that good. I truly have so much to thank Sharon for, but I must share the story of the bags. At the beginning of Boards by Melfran, I ordered a pack of plastic cellophane bags for my crostini, but the night before I needed the cellophane bags, I opened the bags to find out they were mini bags. At ten o'clock, in a panicked state, I texted Sharon to ask if she had any larger cellophane bags. Sure enough, she strolled over, cool as a cucumber, and handed them to me in my frazzled state. I wanted to share one of Sharon's recipes and thought, *What could be better than a recipe for warm, ooey-gooey, cheesy garlic bread?*

Directions

1. Slice French bread loaf in half lengthwise. Place each half, cut side up, on a foil-lined baking sheet. Set aside.

2. Mix softened butter, minced garlic, and 1 tablespoon chopped parsley. Spread evenly on each half of the French bread loaf. In a small bowl, combine cheeses, then sprinkle evenly on top of the bread. Sprinkle remaining parsley evenly over the cheeses.

3. Bake in 350°F (177°C) for 10 minutes. Turn the broiler to high, move the rack up, and broil until cheese starts to turn golden brown.

SWEET & NUTTY CHEVRE

Ingredients

10 oz (284 grams) goat cheese

1 cup (115 grams) unsalted chopped
    walnuts

½ cup (170 grams) honey

Serving Size

3-4 people

It's an interesting story about how this goat cheese came to be. Before it was a sweet and nutty chevre, it was a honey and pomegranate chevre. When I started making boards, my long-time neighbor and family friend requested five large boards for her husband's fortieth birthday. The pressure was on. To alleviate some stress, I decided to get all my groceries earlier in the week so I would have plenty of time to prep, get organized, and feel ready to rock and roll. I bought pomegranate seeds and kept them in the fridge as the label instructed. Fast forward to the morning of the fortieth birthday party. I was moving and grooving until it was time to make my honey and pomegranate goat cheese. I took my pomegranate seeds out of the fridge only to find they were bad. In a panic, I had a feeling maybe I could substitute the pomegranate seeds for chopped walnuts, and here we are. The sweet and nutty chevre was a hit at the fortieth birthday party and has been a highly requested crowd-pleaser ever since. The sweet flavor, smooth texture of the goat cheese, and hint of crunch of the walnuts make a delicious combination. This homemade chevre is a total crowd-pleaser and is always one of the first items demolished on the board.

Directions

1. Finely chop your unsalted walnuts. (You can use a food processor, a knife, or even put the walnuts into a bag and use a rolling pin.)

2. Add all ingredients to a bowl.

3. Mix ingredients until everything is combined.

Styling Tip: Chill the goat cheese for about 30–45 minutes and mold into your desired shape! I like to use cookie cutters to create seasonal shapes, but my go-to is a simple circle.

SPICY HERB CHEVRE

Ingredients

10 oz (283 grams) goat cheese

1–2 tablespoons (5.9 grams) chili flakes (start with one, try it, and add another if you're feeling spicy)

2 tablespoons (4.5 grams) finely chopped basil/dried basil

2 tablespoons (4.5 grams) finely chopped dill/dried dill

2 tablespoons (4.5 grams) finely chopped thyme/dried thyme

2 tablespoons (4.5 grams) finely chopped oregano/dried oregano

2 tablespoons (6 grams) of freshly grated lemon zest (**Be careful zesting**. I do not want to get too graphic, but I may or may not have zested my pinky finger one too many times.)

½ tablespoon (6.5 grams) of olive oil

Serving Size

3-4 people

I have the sweet goat cheese, so naturally, I needed to add some spice. My dad is Indian, so spicy food is his middle name. Funny enough, my mom is not Indian at all—100 percent Caucasian—but she eats spicier foods than my dad. Maybe that makes "spicy" her first name? My friends and family needed something spicy, so I had to comply. This recipe is great because you can play around with the spices and herbs to develop your favorite combination. I like to think of goat cheese as a blank canvas that can be manipulated into almost anything. The recipe is my favorite flavor combination, but please feel free to take creative freedom and adjust it to your taste! The ingredients can all be customized to your liking. This is one recipe you cannot mess up—at least, I do not think you can.

Directions

1. Add all ingredients to a bowl.

2. Mix ingredients until everything is well-combined. The goat cheese should be colorful with all the spices, herbs, and zest.

 Pro Tip: You can mix dry spices and fresh herbs. Fresh herbs add great fragrance and color.

 Styling Tip: Chill the goat cheese for about 30–45 minutes and mold into your desired shape. As per usual, I gravitate toward circles.

THE TAYLOR FAMILY ARTICHOKE DIP

Ingredients

2 cans (480 grams) artichokes in
water, drained

one 8 oz can (227 grams) Ortega chilis

½ cup (115 grams) mayo

½ cup (45 grams) parmesan cheese

1 cup (128 grams) jack cheese

½ teaspoon garlic powder

Salt and pepper to taste

Serving Size

7–9 people

Prior to my charcuterie boards, I think everyone in my family would agree that my mom's artichoke dip was the star appetizer, next to the classic onion dip, of course. This recipe has been in my family forever—well, my mom's family. My mom's maiden name and my middle name are Taylor. You know this recipe is good when it's been a regular at family parties since the 1970s. When I started gathering the recipes for this book, my mom and I stumbled upon the *original* recipe card my nana handwrote (as pictured below). My nana's handwriting is so unique, I can spot it from a mile away—what a blast from the past!

Directions

1. Finely chop the artichokes.

2. Combine the artichokes with the remaining ingredients.

3. Place in an oven-safe dish, preferably a rectangle.

4. Bake for 25 minutes at 350°F (177°C) until melted.

5. Serve with tortilla chips and your favorite crackers.

BOARDS FOR EVERY OCCASION

I can honestly say I have yet to attend any occasion, event, or gathering where a charcuterie board would not have been welcomed with open arms. Since I have unofficially assumed the name Boards by Melfran, I feel it is expected that wherever I am invited, a board will be present. Since the start of Boards by Melfran, there are less than a handful of events or gatherings that I show up to board-less. In fact, for one Thanksgiving, I threw together a last-minute grazing table compiled of leftover scraps. (It still turned out pretty good.)

Pro Tip: Do not throw away your scraps! I guarantee, especially after reading this book, you will be able to throw together something beautiful and delicious. I often refer to these boards as scraps boards or leftovers boards.

My uncle Dave is notorious for his sarcastic sense of humor, though, on the inside, he is the sweetest and most caring uncle a niece could ask for. Let's just say he had some critiques about my Thanksgiving grazing table. Uncle Dave believes that if my name is Boards by Melfran, then all my creations should be on a literal board. When the Thanksgiving charcuterie was on a table (technically parchment paper) instead of a board, he suggested I change my name to Occasional Boards by Melfran. It became the running joke of Thanksgiving, as everyone went to town on the Thanksgiving grazing table. Uncle Dave was unable to let this tragedy go because he proceeded to show up to Christmas dinner with a charcuterie board poem.

Here is his poem:

> A yuletide Charcuterie treat
> Boards by Melfran are rather neat!
> But she makes me swear, my niece doesn't care
> All I get are board-less holiday meats

Here was the board—I mean table—in question:

Anyway, back to the point of this chapter. Every occasion truly deserves a board (or table), and this chapter will help you plan an elegant and seasonal board for the holidays. This chapter focuses on ways to make sure all your party guests, no matter their dietary needs or restrictions, have something beautiful and delicious to enjoy. We all have that one loved one who is dabbling around with the latest diet trend or has food intolerances/preferences that make a charcuterie board challenging. Well, not anymore! I hope this chapter provides you with various ways to accommodate all of your guests with special recipes and creative ideas to make a delicious board for everyone, no matter the celebration—even loved ones with four legs (spoiler alert)!

'Tis the Season

Being the holiday house, everyone has their "assignment." My dad is obviously assigned grilling duties, my mom is assigned all decorating and non-grill preparation, my brother just needs to show up and be nice, and I—well, I ensure everything is seasonal. Before charcuterie boards, I always forced everyone to be seasonal, whether it was gingerbread competitions or Easter egg tosses. Now, the holiday must-have is always a charcuterie board. Family and friends, young and old, all love a charcuterie board. Also, what a great conversation starter for those awkward silences with random family members you haven't seen since the last holiday gathering.

Everyone has their favorite meats, cheese, fruits, and veggies they like on a board. However, the holidays can make it challenging to include vibrant, juicy raspberries on Christmas! My holiday tip is to *never* sacrifice your favorite items for a theme! You can make your board seasonal and fun through shapes, flowers, and details.

Christmas Boards

Christmas time is one of my favorite times of the year, but ironically, I find Christmas boards extremely challenging. Since the main colors of Christmas are red and green, the ability to stick to the theme and use contrasting colors is tough, but we will get through it. My tips and tricks for winter holiday boards include highlighting seasonal items like candy canes, holiday chocolates, candied pecans, and sage.

OH CHRISTMAS TREE, OH CHRISTMAS TREE

Ingredients

8 oz (226 grams) salami

10 oz (283 grams) brie

½ a medium cucumber

1–2 clementines

5–6 oz (142–170 grams) cubed hard cheese

15–20 blackberries

3–4 caprese skewers

2–3 oz (57–85 grams) candied cranberries

8–10 raspberries

1–2 clementine rinds

Serving Size

6–10 people

A Christmas tree is an iconic symbol of the holidays and family time. By making a board into a seasonal shape like a tree, you can effortlessly stay on brand. Keep in mind that you can still include all your favorite board items while remaining seasonal.

Directions

1. Start with a rectangular board, preferably one with edges. (The board pictured about is a twelve-by-sixteen-inch rectangle.)

2. Create your first Christmas tree line with folded salami, leaving space for the trunk.

3. Add slices of brie.

4. Next, add your row of cucumbers.

5. Don't forget the citrus!

6. Add favorite cubed hard cheese.

7. Add blackberries.

8. Add caprese toothpicks (fresh mozzarella, basil, tomato).

9. Add candied cranberries.

10. Add hard salami.

11. Add raspberries.

12. Finally, top with citrus rind stars.

 Style Tip: One of my favorite additions is the citrus rind stars—I'm all about the details!

Valentine's Day Boards

Bring on the hearts—well, the heart-shaped cheese. Valentine's Day colors are deep reds, purples, and pinks, which make for some vibrant boards. Valentine's Day boards are versatile because you can use salami or cucumber roses, heart accents, chocolate-covered strawberries, spell out "Love," or just about anything else you can think of. I have even decorated heart-shaped cookies with sprinkles and frosting and then piled them on a board. Valentine's Day is a unique opportunity to let your love for making boards shine and your creativity flow.

BRIE MINE

Ingredients

21 oz wheel of brie (595 grams)

Serving Size

3-5 people

I feel like I could dedicate a whole chapter to brie because it is so versatile and delicious. Brie is a go-to soft cheese for any board and always a crowd-pleaser. Brie is fantastic to use for holidays because it is the perfect texture to shape with cookie cutters. The ring of the brie ensures the shape will be held, but the gooey, creamy inside makes it moldable and easy to manipulate. By using a heart-shaped cookie cutter, you can add in a heartfelt touch for your galentines, palentines, or your valentine.

Directions

1. Start with a wheel of brie.

2. Place it in the freezer for 5–10 minutes to ensure the center of the brie is nice and firm.

3. Place cookie cutter in the center of the brie, and gently but firmly push down until the cookie cutter is visible on the back side of the brie.

4. Gently push your brie heart out of the wheel.

Styling Tip: Brie is always a winner, but you can use your heart-shaped cookie cutter on fruits with a larger surface area like a kiwi or an orange rind.

Halloween Boards

Time to get spooky! Halloween colors are the obvious black and orange, but since there are so many "characters" on Halloween—like witches, monsters, ghosts, and all the other spooky things—you can carefully select colors that still fit the theme perfectly. I also tie in some minimal fall color accents. Halloween is a fun opportunity to try out garnishes and shapes to create a quirky themed board.

MONSTER MASH

Ingredients

8–10 oz (227–284 grams) goat cheese

5 pitted black olives

1–2 baby colorful carrots

1–2 oz (28–56 grams) brie rind

2 candy eyeball sprinkles

Do not be frightened—it's just spicy goat cheese! Using the spicy herb chevre (pg. 123), I made the monster's face. Depending on how spooky you are going for, you can adjust as needed. When using a fruit or vegetable to create small details, like a mouth and eyes, you will want to keep a few things in mind. First, use something that does not oxidize, like apples or avocados. Second, use a food that is easy to cut but still firm, like an olive. Olives slice easily and hold their shape. Lastly, and maybe one of the most challenging, try to use a fruit or veggie that fits the cheese's flavor profile. For example, if you use the sweet and nutty chevre, using olives to garnish isn't ideal since the chevre is sweet and the olive flavor profile is overpoweringly salty. A better flavor combination would be sweet and nutty chevre with nuts or a berry.

Directions

1. Grab a pliable and moldable cheese. My go-to is goat cheese, specifically the spicy herb chevre (pg. 123).

2. Form your cheese into a square shape. It does not need to be perfect, just spooky.

3. Grab your olives and slice them in halves vertically. Use the halves as ears.

4. Slice another olive horizontally to create round discs to use as eyes.

5. With your leftover rounds, slice them in half and use the lines in alternating diagonal patterns to create a zigzag-like mouth.

6. Place a round of colorful carrots on top of the olive rounds to create a purple iris.

7. Top off the carrot round with a candy eyeball.

8. For the hair, use a rind of brie, cut in a diagonal pattern to mimic hair. Now, you have the most delicious and spooky monster for your board!

Easter Boards

April showers bring May flowers—and Easter colors! Easter colors and spring colors go hand-in-hand. The spring season and Easter holiday are filled with tons of pastels and patterns. During this time of year, I try to garnish with lavender and dried citrus. Try to keep the foods on your board vibrant, and garnish with subtle hints of pastels. To maintain the Easter spirit, I love to use chocolate candy eggs and little chocolate bunnies to change it up. I was always so hesitant to add chocolate to boards, but during my first charcuterie-filled Easter, the chocolate was too cute to resist!

BUNNY DIP

Ingredients

12–16 oz (340–454 grams) hummus

2–3 tablespoons (14 grams) paprika

Serving Size

3–4 people

During Easter time, I like to use the bunny as my signature shape. Trust me; I love Easter eggs—I love an Easter egg toss even more—but unfortunately, since the shape is simply an oval, it requires an insane amount of detail to make it spring-y. The bunny, however, is easily associated with Easter and easy to use. I used a bunny cookie cutter and placed it on top of hummus. Next, I took some paprika and carefully, with a steady hand, sprinkled the paprika inside the cookie cutter to create the cutest little bunny. Aside from hummus and paprika, you can also use any other spread and complementary spice or season.

Pupcuterie

It's Emmy's time to shine! Emmy is the beloved dog behind Boards by Melfran. She enjoys eating, walks, puppy adventures, and puppucinos. My family adopted Emmy from the pound when I was in high school. She is small but has a lot of sass and love to give. I hate to expose Emmy in such a public manner, but it must be done—she has not been the most supportive family member of Boards by Melfran. Creating content and making recipes has dramatically cut into her walking time and, of course, her cuddle time. However, with more thoughtful effort put in on my end, Emmy remains one spoiled and loved dog. Funny enough, Emmy has been able to try many new fruits and vegetables because of Boards by Melfran. Some of Emmy's newly discovered favorite foods are cherries, strawberries, blueberries, and, most of all, cucumbers. Since cucumbers appear on almost every board I create, Emmy has become attuned to the sound cucumbers make when sliced on the cutting board. The moment she hears cucumbers being chopped, she "patiently" waits for her time to munch on the cucumber scraps.

Even though Emmy is the only pup in my eyes, I am fortunate to have many other cute puppers whose favorite foods deserve to be noted. Here is a list of not just Emmy's favorite foods:

Emmy	Rocky	Cooper J	Mindy
• Cucumbers • Strawberries • Cherries • Melon • Spaghetti squash	• Cucumbers • Blueberries • Dumplings (just kidding, one time I was babysitting Rocky's human brother and made dumplings for lunch. I left the dumplings unattended for less than two minutes and returned to no dumplings—it is still a joke to this day.)	• Avocados (eat with caution, Cooper puts on pounds when it is avo season) • Carrots	• American cheese • Chicken • Tortilla chips • Deli meats • Carrots In loving memory of Mindy Novotney.

Emmy

Rocky

Cooper

Mindy

PUPCUTERIE

Ingredients

2–4 oz (57–113 grams) semi-soft
   cheese

6–7 strawberries

3–4 oz (85–113 grams) blueberries

½ of a medium cucumber

6–7 oz (170–198 grams) of your dog's
   favorite treat

3–4 whole colorful carrots

Serving Size

2–3 pups

Directions

1. Place your dog's favorite treat down the middle, accompanied by some bite-size cucumbers.

2. Next up is some colorful carrot curls—gotta keep your dog's eyes at 20/20.

3. Add an assortment of berries so your pup gets fiber, antioxidants, and vitamins.

4. Say cheese! Place sharp cheddar for some protein.

With this combination, you're guaranteed to have one happy dog!

Warning: Please be conscious of the food you provide your pup. Food allergies vary from dog to dog. Be aware that quantity size will also vary from dog to dog. Please double and triple check with a vet to ensure any food you give your dog is safe and edible for them.

Kim-Shin Snack Board

My close family friends are Korean—at this point, we were the Kim-Shin family. I have learned so much about Korean culture from them. I joke that I am part Korean and proceed to show off my knowledge of Korean foods and limited vocabulary. I also learned the art of snacking from them. When I walked into their home, I instantly made myself at home and went straight to their snack drawer. The drawer was always filled with the classics, like biscuit sandwich cookies filled with chocolate, cheddar crackers, and fun, trendy new items like the newest flavor of potato chips or limited-edition chocolate sandwich cookies. It also always had a variety of Asian snacks, like chocolate-covered biscuit sticks. Thus, this board is a collection of our favorite snacks.

Serving Size

4-7 people

Here is what we included on our snack board:

Sour gummy bears

Chocolate-covered gummy bears

Cookie pretzel sticks

Butter crackers

Cheese crackers

Tako chips

Golden cookie thins

Wafers cookies

Peanut butter cups

Obviously, this is our snack board, but I want you to make your snack board with your favorites. When making a snack board, focus on flavor and texture categories. (Expand on flavors and textures of our board.)

If you take a moment to analyze this board through the lens of texture and flavor, choices and options are abundant for all. When making a snack board, it's important to have your favorite items, of course, but make sure you're accommodating your friend with a sweet tooth or your brother who loves chewy textures. Being extremely mindful and thoughtful about a snack board is key because, unlike a charcuterie board, there are not many rational combinations to try together.

For example, you would never find me trying to make my "perfect bite" with cheese crackers and chocolate-covered gummy bears. With a traditional cheese board, you would find me trying a slice of brie with fruit and jam. It is important with any board, but especially this one, to make sure everyone's needs are met—and most (if not all) potential cravings are met, too.

Some rules of thumb I follow when making a fun board, like a snack board, are to have:

- Something you love
- Something you know your guests love
- A guaranteed crowd-pleaser
- Something salty
- Something sweet
- Something crunchy
- Something chewy
- Something new and fun no one has tried

Story Time: In my last year of graduate school, I started to purchase the "new" items from Trader Joe's. I'd bring the new snack of the week to class, and my friends and I would try it out and give our thoughts and overall ratings. This snack of the week became somewhat of a tradition and was always something to look forward to. So, the moral of the story is: Trying new snacks and foods can be a fun and inexpensive bonding activity to do with your friends and family.

GRILLED VEGGIE BOARD

Ingredients

You can truly use whatever vegetables you would like. I used the following:

Eggplant

Zucchini

Tomatoes

Peppers

Asparagus

Red onions

Broccolini

Serving Size

8–10 people

My friend convinced me to take a three-part cooking class. Each class had a three-course meal to prepare. Fun fact: I had the biggest sweet tooth in the world, so I blocked out the other two courses and truly only cared about dessert. Once we got to work, I was informed that one of the side dishes was grilled vegetables. I have had my fair share of grilled veggies, which were pretty good, but I was not too excited. However, these vegetables turned out delicious, and even with my insane sweet tooth, I am always looking for ways to incorporate more vegetables into my diet. After the cooking class, I could not stop thinking about the grilled eggplant and zucchini. The following Sunday, as usual, I headed to the farmers market and grabbed zucchini, eggplant, red onions, peppers, tomatoes, hummus, and tzatziki. That same afternoon, I grabbed a cast iron grill pan because I wanted grill lines. I set it to high heat and turned on the kitchen hood because I recalled the chef stating the heat needed to be high. If you do not have a kitchen hood, the fire alarm will likely go off. Well, the second I put my asparagus on the grill, beep went the fire alarm. Once that crisis was averted, the executive decision was made to move my grilled veggie party outside to the grill. The grill can be an intimidating place, but I set everything up, fired it up, and the remainder of that Sunday was spent grilling up a storm.

 Tzatziki is a yogurt-based spread with cucumbers, garlic, and olive oil. Tzatziki is typically served as a side dish and is light and refreshing.

Directions

1. Slice your long vegetables (zucchini and eggplant) at a 45-degree angle to create more surface area to grill. Slicing straight creates a small surface area.

2. Slice tomatoes and red onions into ¼-inch-thick slices. Be extremely careful not to slice them too thin because the intense heat of the grill will disintegrate the slices.

3. Slice your peppers in half and remove the seeds. Do not cut them more than that, or they can fall through the grill grates.

4. Keep your asparagus and broccolini whole.

5. In 1 cup (225 grams) of olive oil, add:

> 4 minced garlic cloves (or more)
> 3 tablespoons (8 grams) of fresh/dried thyme
> Salt and pepper to taste

6. Let the vegetables marinate for at least 30 minutes. The eggplant and zucchini absorb the most flavor, so let those marinate while you start to grill the other vegetables.

7. Grill until the vegetables are soft and grill lines start to appear. (I prefer my veggies to have a nice char on them, so I let them grill longer.)

8. Plate your veggies with your favorite dips and spreads. I used hummus, tzatziki, and the basil and white bean spread.

Dessert Board

Confession: As previously mentioned, I have a sweet tooth. I always have, and I am convinced I always will. Despite the abundance of desserts that exist, my heart belongs to chocolate. Naturally, both these boards are packed with chocolate. Everyone needs a little sweetness in life, and it's such an out-of-the-box way to enjoy dessert at your next gathering. If you need a dessert that lets everyone have a little something or you are craving something sweet, these two boards are for you.

Chocolate hummus is the new chocolate-covered strawberry that makes life a lot easier and just as delicious. Heavy whipping cream goes great with just about any fruit you can think of. Start by gathering 2–3 of your favorite cookies, add your dips, and fill in with fruit. Your cookies will serve as your "crackers," and from there, you can mix and match your spreads and fruits.

On this board, I used:

Chocolate hummus

Whipped cream

Madeleine cookies

Palmier cookies

Grapes

Cherries

Raspberries

Blackberries

Blueberries

S'mores Board

When I think of s'mores, many fond memories come to mind. I think of my family and friends all huddled around the fire pit after a BBQ. This board is beyond interactive and customizable. It utilizes a portable campfire, but of course, any type of fire (as long as it's safe) will work. When making this board, think outside the box and get creative with the "vehicle" for the s'mores. Keeping it traditional, of course, graham crackers make an appearance. Next up, we have Funfetti chewy cookies and chocolate sandwich cookies. Once we have the vehicle down, add in something meltable. I chose to use peanut butter cups and chocolate bars. You can also use peppermint patties or chocolate-covered caramels. Now, it's time for the dipping and spreading. I used hazelnut spread, peanut butter (smooth, not crunchy), and caramel. Oh, and don't forget the marshmallows!

Crudités Board

Everyone deserves hap-pea-ness! This board, without a doubt, will lettuce turnip that beet! Enough with the puns, thyme to get to the crudités!

Focus on your dips and spreads. Veggies pack a crunch, so accompanying that crunch with a creamy, flavorful spread is the way to go. Sun spread (pg. 108), hummus, and spreadable goat cheese are all great options to pair with your favorite crudités. Naturally, with a veggie board, the focus is meatless, so bring on the cheese. Try to limit the hard cheese because you are providing so many crunchy, firm textures with veggies. Stick to soft, creamy, spreadable cheeses to give your board variety. Stick to your classic favorite vegetables like cucumber, broccoli, and carrots. Do not be afraid to spice it up using out-of-the-box vegetables, like endives and radishes. Traditionally, since crudités means raw vegetables, veggies are the focus, but fruit is always welcome—your board, your rules!

Here is a list of ingredients that I typically use for a crudités board:

> 1 medium cucumber
> 12–16 oz (340–454 grams) hummus
> 3 oz (85 grams) petite colorful carrots
> 7 oz (198 grams) endives
> 12–16 oz (340–454 grams) Sun Spread (pg. 108)

Styling Tip: To spice things up, add a personal touch to your board with a cucumber rose.

Tea Time

I inherited my love for vintage antiques from my nana. Her home is filled with beautiful pieces of the past—one item being teacups. As a child, I spent many afternoons antiquing with Nana in small beachside shops. Learning to appreciate the past from a young age has shaped me into the person I am today. Some of my best memories growing up were getting all dolled up and heading to the British specialty shop by my house for a tea party with my mom, grandmas, and aunts. I have tried to incorporate tea parties into my adult life as much as possible. In fact, I had a tea-quila-themed birthday party where everyone drank margaritas out of teacups. One afternoon, I was hanging out with Nana and checking out her teacups when it hit me—why not make charcuterie teacups? Tea parties are fun for anyone of any age, and what is a better way to elevate your next tea party than with a personal teacup full of charcuterie?

In my teacup, I included the following:

Salami rose
Irish cheddar
Blueberries
Raspberries
Blackberries
Clementines

Fruit Board

A fruit board is a fun and fantastic way to get lots of extra vitamins and antioxidants. I cannot pretend I was 1,000 percent healthy while enjoying this because chocolate croissants and some champagne accompanied this board, but my daily fruit serving was fulfilled. A fruit board is perfect for a breakfast, brunch, or even a midday snack on a hot summer day.

Fruit boards are full of color and are an innovative way to try new fruits. This board was the first time I tried yellow dragon fruit, which was delicious. Make sure to be conscious of fruits that may oxidize once they are cut. For instance, on this board, I added the bananas last to make sure they did not turn brown (**Pro Tip!**).

For the board, I used the following fruits:

Yellow dragon fruit

Kiwi

Pineapple

Kumquats

Banana

Blueberries

Strawberries

Raspberries

Styling Tip: Sharpen your knives and try out some innovative ways to cut your fruit. Take a fruit like a kiwi (I also will use this technique on strawberries, oranges, and even blueberries) and make a small diagonal cut in the middle of the fruit. For the next cut, alternate the direction of the diagonal line and continue in that pattern until your fruit is sliced.

BREAKFAST BOARD

Ingredients

4–6 croissants

Seeds of one pomegranate

8 oz (227 grams) strawberries

6 oz (170 grams) raspberries

6 oz (170 grams) blueberries

1 medium orange

8 oz (227 grams) bacon

10–12 mini sausage links

8–10 hash browns

8 oz (227 grams) yogurt

Serving Size

4-5 people

Breakfast is the most important meal of the day and notably one of my favorite meals. I say "favorite" with caution because for breakfast to be my favorite meal it needs to be a *good* breakfast. Having cereal with milk does not cut it for me—I do not even like milk in my cereal. A breakfast board is a fun spin on your classic board. For my breakfast boards, I always make sure there is a great balance of sweet and savory. I enjoy including various fresh and seasonal fruits and hearty carbs like croissants, cinnamon rolls, pancakes, or waffles. For salty items, I love an extra crispy hash brown topped with a sprinkle of pink Himalayan salt, turkey bacon, and sausage. You can add something fun like Greek yogurt, oatmeal, or spreads like jam or peanut butter.

CLOSING TIME

We have unfortunately reached the end of the book. I hope you feel empowered, inspired, and eager to make beautiful memories. Remember to trust your intuition and embrace your creativity. Practicing a skill or recipe is key to success and building your confidence as the chef and host you are meant to be. Creating boards and bites should be a fun, creative outlet for you, and I hope this book has assisted you on your chef journey. Thank you so much for being a part of my own creative journey—I truly hope you have learned a handful of tips, tricks, and recipes that will become staples in your life.

P.S.

I hope this book has made you smile, empowered you, and helped you create memories to share surrounded by loved ones and an abundant board.

ACKNOWLEDGMENTS

There are not enough synonyms for "thank you" for this section, so I apologize for the repetition of the words "thank you."

I am extremely thankful for many people. I am beyond fortunate to have encountered the most supportive and encouraging souls. My parents are two of the most selfless, hardworking, and dedicated people. They have supported me during any tragedy, triumph, and dream (except my dream to be a ceramicist). My grandparents have done nothing but encourage me and hype me up every step of the way. A huge thank you to my uncle Dave, the photo genius and author of the lovely poem on page 127. Uncle Dave converted every photo in this book to the correct format and made color corrections. This book is a compilation of my entire family's hard work and support.

An extremely special thank you to my friends, the whole reason the Instagram page Boards by Melfran was created. We all had a wine night, I made a board, and the next day the @boardsbymelfran Instagram was born. Thank you to everyone who came over for a "picnic" or "dinner party" that turned into a content-creation hangout. I am a needy friend who requires feedback, consulting, and constant reassurance. I am forever grateful to them for providing me that—you know who you are. A special thank you to one of my dearest friends, Emane Henderson, for creating the graphics for this book and working with my ever-evolving vision.

Thank you to my coworkers, supervisors, and professors who have shown me an overwhelming amount of support, not only with Boards by Melfran but also with my career. Thank you to all my students, patients, and the people I have worked with who show me how far determination, positivity, and hard work can get you.

A humongous thank you to the team at Mango Publishing. Many thanks to Natasha Vera, who believed in me and reached out in the first place. This book all started with an Instagram DM, and now we are here. Thank you to Julianna Holshue for answering my million questions and three-in-the-morning emails during this process.

Honestly, I like to think that almost everyone in my life has impacted me as a human and this book as a byproduct.

To my readers, thank you for choosing this book, and I hope it has exceeded all your expectations. Thank you all for the overwhelming love, support, and positivity you have provided in my life.

ABOUT THE AUTHOR

Melissa Francis, better known as "Melfran" (an endearing combination of her first and last name), is the face behind the board and book. In January 2020, she made her first charcuterie board, and charcuterie boards became her creative outlet and a way to bring family and friends together. Ever since her first board, she's been hooked, and honestly, so has everyone else!

As a child, Melissa loved arts and crafts. She truly thought she was "the best artist in the world," just like her nana told her. As she grew older, she dabbled in jewelry-making and cooking classes, and "thrived" (in her opinion) in high school ceramics. She always gravitated toward artistic activities and loved cooking. With only so many hours in the day, she mainly spent time playing soccer and focused on trying to find a career.

In 2014, she attended California State Polytechnic University, Pomona, to play soccer. However, that did not go as planned. Plot twist: she joined a sorority and decided to major in psychology. While exploring career paths, she fell in love with the field of speech and language pathology. Melissa received her master of science from Chapman University in communication sciences and disorders in 2021. She is currently a practicing speech and language pathologist and loves what she does and the individuals she works with.

Melissa is the content creator behind @boardsbymefran and the author of *Boards & Bites*.

yellow pear 🍐 press

Yellow Pear Press, established in 2015, publishes inspiring, charming, clever, distinctive, playful, imaginative, beautifully designed lifestyle books, cookbooks, literary fiction, notecards, and journals with a certain *joie de vivre* in both content and style. Yellow Pear Press books have been honored by the Independent Publisher Book (IPPY) Awards, National Indie Excellence Awards, Independent Press Awards, and International Book Awards. Reviews of our titles have appeared in Kirkus Reviews, Foreword Reviews, Booklist, Midwest Book Review, San Francisco Chronicle, and New York Journal of Books, among others. Yellow Pear Press joined forces with Mango Publishing in 2020, with the vision to continue publishing clever and innovative books. The fact that they're both named after fruit is a total coincidence.

We love hearing from our readers, so please stay in touch with us and follow us at:

Facebook: Mango Publishing
Twitter: @MangoPublishing
Instagram: @MangoPublishing
LinkedIn: Mango Publishing
Pinterest: Mango Publishing

Newsletter: mangopublishinggroup.com/newsletter